W 5029141 6

A DIALOGUE WIT[H]
ALBERT ELLIS

AF791552

WESTHILL COLLEGE LIBRARY

Weoley Park Road
Birmingham B29 6LL
Tel: 021-472 7245

A fine will be charged if this book is returned after the last date stamped below.

11 NOV 1994
- 9 DEC 1994
20 JAN 1995
24 MAR 1995
23 NOV 1995
-8. NOV. 1996
-6. DEC. 1996
18 JAN 1999
28 APR 1999
10 JAN 2001
12. NOV. 1997
30 SEP 1999
18 NOV 1999
7 Feb 2001
8 JUN 2001
20 DEC 2002
13 JAN 2003
-4 FEB 2008

THERAPEUTICALLY SPEAKING SERIES
Series editor: Windy Dryden

TITLES IN THE SERIES

Published titles

Windy Dryden: *A Dialogue with Albert Ellis*
Windy Dryden: *A Dialogue with Arnold Lazarus*
Windy Dryden: *A Dialogue with John Norcross*

A DIALOGUE WITH ALBERT ELLIS

Against Dogma

WINDY DRYDEN

OPEN UNIVERSITY PRESS
Milton Keynes · Philadelphia

Open University Press
Celtic Court
22 Ballmoor
Buckingham
MK18 1XW

and
1900 Frost Road, Suite 101
Bristol, PA 19007, USA

First Published 1991

Copyright © Windy Dryden and Albert Ellis 1991

All rights reserved. No part of this publication may be reproduced, stored in a retrieval system or transmitted in any form or by any means, without written permission from the publisher.

British Library Cataloguing-in-Publication Data

Dryden, Windy
A dialogue with Albert Ellis: Against dogma.
– (Therapeutically speaking series)
I. Title. II. Series
616.89

ISBN 0–335–09286–1
ISBN 0–335–09285–3 (pbk)

Library of Congress Cataloging-in-Publication Data

Dryden, Windy.
A dialogue with Albert Ellis/Windy Dryden.
p. cm. – (Therapeutically speaking series)
Includes bibliographical references and index.
ISBN 0–335–09286–1 – ISBN 0–335–09285–3 (pbk.)
1. Psychotherapy. 2. Ellis, Albert – Interviews.
I. Ellis, Albert. II. Title. III. Series.
RC480.5.D78 1991
616.89'14–dc20 91–9732
CIP

Typeset by Type Study, Scarborough, North Yorkshire
Printed in Great Britain by
J. W. Arrowsmith Limited, Bristol

This book is dedicated to the
memory of Peva Keane

WESTHILL COLLEGE LIBRARY
WJ0291416
19.4.94
00376-£12.99
616.8914
DRY

CONTENTS

PREFACE

The purpose of this series is to explore the ideas of established and emerging leaders in the field of psychotherapy. The interview format was chosen to give the 'feel' of an informal but disciplined discussion of each expert's ideas. It is hoped that the books convey the sense of two colleagues engaged in a searching discussion of the ideas of one of them.

The development of the books followed a standard pattern. Initially, I negotiated with the persons concerned the content of each set of interviews. The experts were given the choice of preparing as much or as little material as they wanted in advance of the interviews. Then the interviews were conducted and transcribed. Finally, both I and the interviewees went over the interviews, tidying up the English, with the latter adding or deleting material as they saw fit. In general, however each book remains faithful to the interviews as they were conducted.

Windy Dryden

1 INTRODUCTION

Albert Ellis was born in Pittsburgh, America, on 13 September 1913. He began his career as a psychotherapist by using self-help techniques on himself. He was anxious and shy as a child and early adolescent, suffered severely from insomnia, was extremely phobic about all kinds of public speaking, and was highly sexual in his desires but completely inhibited heterosexually. Being an avid reader from his sixth year onward, he sought self-help materials in fictional and non-fictional writings. This tendency accelerated at the age of 16, when he became primarily interested in philosophy, especially the philosophy of human happiness. By the time he was 20, he had read almost all the great philosophers and psychologists of that day (1933) and applied many of their writings to his own neurotic problems. He was especially influenced by Epicurus, Epictetus, Marcus Aurelius, Spinoza, Kant, Emerson, Thoreau and Russell and by Freud, Adler, Jung and Watson. In his twenties he also read a number of self-help books, especially Emile Coué's writings on autosuggestion.

Motivated by his philosophical and psychological reading, and by his early determination to overcome his own anxieties and inhibitions, Ellis began, around the age of 19, to do some serious *in vivo* desensitization on himself; within a few years, he was able to quite successfully overcome his insomnia, his public-speaking phobia, and his sexual inhibition. He therefore became interested in writing on the philosophy of human happiness and in his mid-twenties actually wrote a manuscript, which never got published, 'The art of never making yourself desperately unhappy'. At this time his main ambition was to be a successful writer of fiction and non-fiction, but when he failed to get anywhere with the stories, novels, plays and comic poems that he kept writing, he decided to concentrate on non-fiction – especially on writing about sex, love and marriage. He assumed – not necessarily correctly! – that this kind of writing would be more attractive to publishers and readers; he also had a great interest in spreading some of his own quite liberal views on sex and love to the ready populace.

Being an almost compulsive researcher, Ellis read literally hundreds of articles and books on sex, love and marriage and became so much of an expert in these areas that his friends and their friends soon began flocking to him for counselling about their own problems. Though he had only a Bachelor of Business Administration degree, he found to his surprise that in talking with these volunteer clients only a few times, he was usually able to help them resolve their sex problems and even some of their important love and marital difficulties.

Ellis also discovered that he greatly enjoyed doing counselling and decided to make it, along with writing, his main career. Because there were no graduate degrees at that time in sex or marital therapy, he decided to start taking a degree (when he was 28) in clinical psychology at Teachers College, Columbia University. He did very well in his graduate work, published a seminal and widely quoted paper, 'The sexual psychology of human hermaphrodites' (Ellis 1945), and collected all his data and was about to write his PhD dissertation on the love relationships of young women when he was informed that two influential professors were unalterably opposed to his doing *any* kind of a thesis on sex or love, and that they would sabotage him at the final defence of his dissertation.

Refusing to make himself desperately unhappy about this great frustration, and using some of the techniques he had outlined in his own unpublished book on minimizing misery, Ellis quickly produced and passed his orals on a second, deliberately non-controversial and highly statistical dissertation, 'A comparison of the use of direct and indirect phrasing in personality questionnaires'. Once again, he did such extensive and intensive research in this area that he published, mostly while he was still in graduate school, almost a dozen papers and monographs on personality tests, including a long and widely quoted review, 'The validity of personality questionnaires', that was published in the *Psychological Bulletin* (Ellis 1946), then the main American Psychological Association journal. For the next few years, Ellis became one of the leading authorities in the world on personality tests and was asked to write a number of other papers on that subject.

Ellis, however, found paper and pencil as well as projective personality tests relatively boring compared to his psychotherapeutic endeavours and abandoned them for clinical and research work in sex and love. After obtaining his MA in clinical psychology in 1943, he started a private practice of general sex and marital therapy; after he received his PhD degree in 1947, he extended this practice and wrote a number of professional and popular articles in these areas. He also started to give many scientific and popular talks and workshops on sex and love; he became so well known that he was asked by Charles Boni, a famous liberal publisher of that day, to write his first published book, *The Folklore of Sex* (Ellis 1951).

During the next fifteen years Ellis became, next to Kinsey, probably the USA's leading sexologist. Moreover, where Kinsey and his collaborators stayed strictly with research data and professional writings, Ellis published several popular books, including *Sex without Guilt* (Ellis 1958), *The Art and Science of Love* (Ellis 1960), *Sex and the Single Man* (Ellis 1963a), and *The Intelligent Woman's Guide to Manhunting* (Ellis 1963b). All these books, and a number of his other popular works on sex and love, went into best-selling paperback editions. By the time the famous sex revolution of the 1960s got underway, he had become one of its main promulgators and leaders.

Ellis was also a pioneering sex therapist. He had no formal training in this area – because such training did not exist when he first started to practise sex and marital therapy in 1943 – but he learned to do so by reading Havelock Ellis, Iwan Bloch, August Forel, W. F. Robie, Victor Robinson, T. H. Van de Velde and other sexologists, most of whom were physicians and who treated people with sex problems with active-directive counselling. After very wide reading in the field, and after early experimental counselling of his own, Ellis became a leading sex therapist and writer, who particularly upheld the views that masturbation was a very good and healthy act, especially for women who had difficulty coming to orgasm. He became well known as a psychologist who was really enthusiastic about masturbation and who showed people – especially women – how to masturbate guiltlessly in order to achieve sex satisfaction and to learn how they could then come to orgasm in heterosexual and homosexual relations.

Ellis, along with Kinsey and G. Lombard Kelly, also became noted for encouraging people to desacredize intercourse, and to see sex as any form of mutually agreed upon stimulation, and not mainly as a penile-vaginal intercourse (Ellis 1953). He was often strongly criticized for his sexual liberalism, as well as for his early advocacy of gay liberation and his active participation in the defence of several individuals who were being legally persecuted for their homosexual behaviour (Ellis 1952; Ellis and Cory 1952). Because of his sexual liberalism, he was one of the few non-homosexuals to be made an honorary member of the first gay liberation group, the Mattachine Society.

When he started to practise rational-emotive therapy (RET), at the beginning of 1955, Ellis found that it was ideally suited to sex, love and marital therapy and gave talks and wrote papers showing that sex therapists had better deal not *only* with their clients' sexual difficulties but also with their *general* disturbances. Unlike Freud, who believed that people's neuroses stemmed from their sex problems, Ellis came to see that the sexual anxieties and inadequacies largely stemmed from their general neurotic demands – from their insistence that they absolutely *must* perform well sexually (and otherwise), *had* to please their partners, and *should* have good love and marital relations. With his sex therapy cases, therefore, he always combined RET with the regular sex education he had previously done; with his clients with general disturbances he often included, where applicable, some sex, love and marital therapy. He thus became, starting in 1943, one of the pioneer marriage and family therapists in the USA. Being something of a propagandist, and from the start seeing psychotherapy as a mode of education that could be taught to the whole populace, rather than to a few psychotherapy clients, he began a professional and a public campaign to convince the world that sex was good for, by, and of itself – though it might very well be better when allied with other human relations, such as love or marriage – and that it did not have to be tied to other aspects of human relationships in order to be good or legitimate.

While he was becoming a notable sex therapist, Ellis was trying to devise a more efficient method of psychotherapy. From 1943 to 1947 he was mainly psychoanalytic, though hardly Freudian, and in 1947 he decided to get some real status in this field and to be analysed himself and to do control work with a training analyst of the Karen Horney Institute, Dr Charles Hulbeck. Because Hulbeck had been a Freudian analyst in Berlin for twenty-five years before he came to the USA, he used the classical technique of free association, dream analysis and silent listening. His final interpretations, however, were neo-Freudian and existentialist.

Ellis enjoyed his analysis but had only one major problem to work on: his compulsively working to complete everything possible in very short periods of time. By talking to Hulbeck about this and giving thought to it himself, he decided that by the time he died he would still have fifty or more books unfinished – and that was all right.

Otherwise, as Hulbeck pointed out, he had largely analysed himself before he entered therapy, and was dealing with the complexities of his life in an unanxious and undepressed manner.

While he was working with Hulbeck, particularly as a trainee, for four years, Ellis did classical analysis with most of his clients; then, finding that inefficient, switched mainly to psychoanalytically oriented psychotherapy. But that, too, he found quite inefficient and unscientific. Between 1947 and 1950 he published several papers attempting to show psychoanalysts how to be more efficient and scientific, culminating in his widely read monograph, 'An introduction to the principles of scientific psychoanalysis' (Ellis 1950).

Although these papers were well received and quoted by leading anti-analysts, they were almost totally ignored and reviled by the psychoanalytic profession. This, along with his continual experimentation with analytic technique, helped Ellis to see that psychoanalysis probably could not be saved. So in 1953 he turned against analysis: he began to speak against it and to call himself a psychotherapist instead of a psychoanalyst.

In 1953 he also started carrying out extensive research for a monograph, 'New approaches to psychotherapy techniques' (Ellis 1955), in which he reviewed scores of cognitive, behavioural and emotive techniques. He experimented with many of these methods, discarded most of them as ineffective or iatrogenic, and combined what he considered the best of them in RET, which he started to do – and at first called rational therapy (RT) – in the beginning of 1955.

From 1955 onward, Ellis made the growth and development of RET his prime interest. His first book on the subject, *How to Live with a Neurotic*, was written in the course of a few weeks in 1955 and published in 1957; his first paper on RET was given at the American Psychological Association convention in Chicago in 1956 and published in 1958. At this time he also started writing a number of other public and professional papers and giving many talks on RET to the public and the profession. He met with enormous opposition from almost all other schools of therapy – from psychoanalytic, client-centred, experiential and behaviour therapists – most of whom considered him to be too direct, too cognitive and too simplistic. Among a few leading therapists who favoured his work were Rudolf Dreikurs, Frederick Thorne and Harry Bone. Rollo May thought him 'too controversial' but sent him some difficult clients whom May chose not to therapize with his much more passive existential approach. Along with May, there were several other leading therapists whom he knew personally who heavily opposed him – including Fritz Perls, Carl Rogers, Carl Whitaker, O. Hobart Mowrer and Joseph Wolpe.

Nothing daunted, Ellis continued to plug away for the third modern revolution that he favoured. From his nineteenth to his twenty-third year, he was a political revolutionist, and for one year actually a paid revolutionist, quite opposed to the US Communist party but none the less a communist with a small 'c'. But he then decided that communist states were almost inevitably fascistic and anti-democratic, and would *not* wither away (as Lenin said they would). So he gave up political revolution and started to work for a sex revolution. While doing quite well in that respect, he realized that the psychotherapy of his day, which he thought was nauseatingly psychoanalytic and anti-scientific, could also benefit from a revolutionary scientific approach. So, true to his natural sceptical and revolutionary tendencies, he started to criticize orthodox psychoanalysis and wrote several papers on this theme, particularly his monograph, 'An introduction to the principles of scientific psychoanalysis' (Ellis 1950). Even after he created RET, he continued to promote it in a highly active manner, and to keep revising and updating it in significant ways.

Ellis continued to work with RET in his own large clinical practice in New York from1955 to 1970 and to add various techniques to his RET armamentarium – particularly emotive methods. In the late 1960s he watched William Schutz in action and used one of his associates to learn the fundamentals of experiential exercises and encounter therapy. He didn't hesitate to combine these exercises with RET and even invented some of his own experiential and emotive techniques – especially his famous shame-attacking exercise, which many other regular and experiential therapists then began to copy. Ellis started using a good many experiential exercises in his regular therapy groups and in many fourteen to twenty-four hour marathons that he gave in New York and in other cities. In the 1960s too, Ellis added many behavioural methods to RET, so that it became a truly multimodal form of treatment several years before Arnold Lazarus originated multimodal therapy.

Until the late 1960s Ellis and his followers were virtually the only pioneering cognitive-behavioural therapists. But as the 1970s got underway, he was joined by several other cognitive-behaviourists, including William Glasser (1965), Aaron Beck (1967), Albert Bandura (1969), Maxie Maultsby (1971), Arnold Lazarus (1971), Donald Meichenbaum (1971), Michael Mahoney (1974), Victor Raimy

(1975), and Marvin Goldfried and Gerald Davison (1976). Several of these cognitive-behaviourists and their students started to do outcome studies showing that this form of therapy produced remarkably good results; by the approach of the 1980s cognitive-behaviour therapy was exceptionally popular as a school in its own right and as the advocate of a number of cognitive methods that began to be incorporated into several other popular schools of therapy. Some of the new cognitive-behavioural schools claimed to have originated their own brands of therapy, but any sophisticated reader of the psychological literature can easily see that they would probably never have started without their being aware of the pioneering work and strong proselytizing efforts of Albert Ellis. Because of these efforts, particularly between 1955 and 1965, Ellis can accurately be called the father of rational-emotive therapy (RET) and the grandfather of cognitive-behaviour therapy (CBT).

It is notable in this respect that had Ellis not strongly used some elements of RET on himself, he probably would not have succeeded in his pioneering endeavours in the fields of sex and psychotherapy. Since the beginning of the 1950s, he has often been powerfully opposed, reviled and censored for his revolutionary views. As a result of refusing to recant some of his liberal sex and unconventional psychotherapy positions, he lost his job as chief psychologist of the State of New Jersey; was falsely accused of unethical sexual practices (such as having heterosexual and homosexual relations with his clients); was refused teaching positions at leading universities (including his own graduate school, Teachers College, Columbia University); was banned from several leading radio and TV programmes (especially the Johnny Carson Show); had some of his books (particularly *Sex without Guilt* and *The Art and Science of Love*) banned from public sale and from newspaper and magazine advertising; lost the presidency of several professional associations that his stature as a psychologist would have otherwise easily earned for him; was refused publication by a number of professional and popular periodicals; had talks and workshops cancelled or banned at several leading universities (notably the University of Arkansas); was investigated by the FBI for his political and his sex views; was refused membership or fellowship in some professional associations (such as the American Psychopathology Association); was picketed and reviled by several anti-sexual organizations (particularly in Oklahoma City when he was a keynote speaker for the Southwestern Psychological Association); had his contracts for books cancelled by leading publishers (notably by Doubleday); was threatened with physical harm by ultra-conservative groups; and suffered other kinds of harassment, reviling and censorship for his outspoken opposition to conventional sexual and psychotherapeutic positions.

Although he was keenly disappointed when these attacks and discriminations against him were made, and although he often determinedly fought back against them, Ellis never seriously depressed or angered himself, never damned nor acted vindictively against his violent detractors and false accusers, and steadfastly continued to promulgate heretical views. People often guessed that he was not disturbed about calumnious and widespread opposition because he was successful with many professionals and members of the public. But his reply was that he was successful because of his lack of disturbance about this opposition. In any event, it seems clear that since starting to fashion the principles and practice of RET in 1953, he has nicely used them on himself to help himself, as one of the titles of one of his main popular books says, *How to Stubbornly Refuse to Make Yourself Miserable About Anything – Yes, Anything!* (Ellis 1988).

While promulgating and pushing RET and sexual liberalism, Ellis was also quite active in several professional organizations, especially the American Psychological Association, in which he has served on several committees and councils, has been president of its Division of Consulting Psychology, and has helped found its Division of Psychotherapy and Division of Humanistic Psychology. In the 1950s he was the main founder (and first president) of the Society for a Scientific Study of Sex and also the most active founder (and vice president) of the American Academy of Psychotherapists. In the 1960s he also helped found and was a leading committee and board member of the American Association of Sex Educators, Counselors and Therapists. He has received Distinguished Awards from all these associations, as well as from the American Humanist Association, and the American Association for Counseling and Development, and the National Academy of Practice. In the 1980s three surveys of psychologists, counsellors and marriage and family therapists showed him to be among the very top influential and most cited writers in these fields.

Ellis has continued to write popular books on RET up to the present day. These have almost all gone into paperback reprints and have sold millions of copies – especially *How to Live with a Neurotic* (Ellis 1957); *Humanistic Psychotherapy* (Ellis 1973a); *A New Guide to Rational Living* (Ellis and Harper 1975); *Anger – How to Live With and Without it* (Ellis 1977a); *A Guide to Personal Happiness* (Ellis and Becker 1982); and *How to Stubbornly Refuse to Make Yourself Miserable about Anything – Yes, Anything!* (Ellis 1988). These have been translated into about twenty different languages; they have been copied, with or without giving Ellis credit, by innumerable other writers of self-help books. In fact, the Ellis- influenced self-help books have so saturated the market that Ellis himself has trouble getting his own popular RET books accepted by a large publisher today!

Ellis has also made many popular recorded audio and video cassettes for the Institute for Rational-Emotive Therapy, for *Psychology Today*, and for several other organizations. Some of his most popular audio cassettes include, *Conquering Low Frustration Tolerance* (Ellis 1972a); *How to Stubbornly Refuse to be Ashamed of Anything* (Ellis 1973b); *Twenty-One Ways to Stop Worrying* (Ellis 1973c); *Conquering the Dire Need for Love* (Ellis 1977b); *A Garland of Rational Songs* (Ellis 1977c); and *Effective Self-Assertion* (Ellis 1986).

Professionally, Ellis has also continued to turn out about fifteen articles and one or two books every year. Some of his recent books include *The Practice of Rational-Emotive Therapy* (Ellis and Dryden 1987); *Rational-Emotive Therapy with Alcoholics and Substance Abusers* (Ellis et al. 1988); *Rational-Emotive Couples Therapy* (Ellis et al. 1989); and *Why Some Therapies don't Work: The Dangers of Transpersonal Psychology* (Ellis and Yeager 1989).

Many articles and books about Ellis and RET also continue to be published. Some of the recent ones are *Albert Ellis: Passionate Skeptic* (Wiener 1988); *Profile of Psychologist Albert Ellis* (Warga 1988); *Inside Rational-Emotive Therapy* (Bernard and DiGiuseppe 1989); 'Albert Ellis: An efficient and passionate life' (Dryden 1989); *Will the Real Albert Ellis Please Stand Up?* (DiMattia and Lega 1990); and *Doing RET: Albert Ellis in Action* (Yankura and Dryden 1990).

Ellis continues to gather acclaim (and calumny!) to this day. After neglecting him for many years, his undergraduate college, the City College of New York, and his graduate university, Teachers College, Columbia University, both gave him Distinguished Alumni Awards. The American Association for Mental Health Counselors signally honoured him by devoting their entire 1990 Annual Conference in Keystone, Colorado, to him and to RET.

Now in his seventy-ninth year, Ellis maintains his exceptionally busy activities in psychology, just as he has for almost the last half-century. At the Institute for Rational-Emotive Therapy in New York, he sees eighty or more individual therapy clients each week, as well as leads five therapy group sessions. He supervises a dozen therapists and interns, conducts his famous regular Friday Night Workshops for the public, and gives numerous talks and workshops at the Institute and for other New York organizations. Most of the weeks of the year he also gives one or two out-of-town talks and workshops, mainly in the USA, but also frequently abroad, in the course of which he gives about 200 public therapy demonstrations. He participates in about ten training practica for the Institute each year, in the course of which he lectures to, demonstrates for, and supervises the recorded therapy sessions of about 150 American and foreign candidates for RET training certificates. Does Ellis have indefatigable energy in performing all these clinical and writing activities in his late seventies, even though he has suffered from diabetes since the age of 40? As he says, 'Not quite, but almost!'

As noted above, Ellis has always kept revising and adding to the theory and practice of RET and is still busy in this respect. Though he and thousands of other cognitive-behaviourists throughout the world still largely follow his original formulations, as presented in *Reason and Emotion in Psychotherapy* (Ellis 1962), some of his more recent formulations are presented in this book. Ellis says that he plans to keep working with and revising RET for his remaining years until he dies in the saddle, which I hope will be a very long time in the future.

1 MAJOR THEORETICAL PRINCIPLES

WINDY DRYDEN In this first interview, I want to go over some of the major theoretical principles that underlie your approach to psychotherapy, so perhaps we can start with the first one.

ALBERT ELLIS The first Rational-Emotive Therapy (RET) principle is that people do not get upset from conditions, circumstances and their early childhood, but that most of them are born with a strong tendency to upset themselves, and to blame their upsetness on the environment, parents and others. But if they acknowledge that they largely, though not completely, tend to upset *themselves*, they can see exactly what they do to create their disturbances and can minimize their upsetness. They can stubbornly refuse to make themselves miserable – that is severely anxious and depressed – about anything. They are born and reared with *two* conflicting tendencies: one, to foolishly defeat themselves and make themselves neurotic; and two, to creatively and constructively change and actualize themselves.

W.D. You mentioned that you hypothesize that people are born with a tendency to upset themselves.

A.E. Right.

W.D. Now, what evidence do you have to back up that statement?

A.E. Well, I have a whole article on this (Ellis 1976) which gives many pieces of evidence why I think that people largely disturb themselves, and let me just outline a few of them right now. One is that virtually all humans, no matter how bright and educated they are, and by whom they were raised, or in what country or with what religion, do very frequently upset themselves. That seems to be human nature, and that includes psychotherapists. Even when people are therapists or psychologists, social workers or psychiatrists, they frequently needlessly upset themselves. Even when you know RET and you *know* that you largely upset yourself, and you clearly see how you do so, you still have great difficulty, quite frequently – I would say usually – in un-upsetting yourself.

Another piece of evidence is that when you have therapy – self-therapy or regular therapy – for an emotional disturbance or problem, and you improve, so that you are no longer terribly anxious or depressed or enraged, you frequently fall back to neurotic behaviour. It seems to be very easy to do so, even after years of therapy.

Also, whenever people encounter unfortunate conditions – for instance, harsh criticism, crises or accidents – they often seem to jump from what we call *appropriate* negative feelings, which help them overcome those conditions, such as sorrow and regret and frustration and annoyance, to *in*appropriate, self-defeating feelings which make them cope poorly. Almost all people frequently make themselves terribly anxious and depressed and then behave worse than they would if they experienced appropriate negative feelings, such as concern and displeasure.

Another thing that I have observed in RET for years and that some other therapists, such as Paul Watzlawick and others, have observed from a slightly different standpoint, is that when people try to solve a practical problem like a marital problem or a work problem, they very frequently pick the wrong solution to the problem. They seem to have a genius for picking a so-called solution that really won't work.

A classic example is those people who are afraid to go in elevators. That's a practical problem, so you would think they would figure out on their own – and we're talking about bright and educated people now – that the obvious thing to do would be to go in elevators, elevators and more elevators, in order to overcome their phobia. Also, those people who are terrified of public speaking – the obvious thing would be for them to keep speaking in public so that they would get less afraid and get better at speaking. But these people often develop severe phobias and withdraw from facing elevators or public speaking, and their avoidance makes them more afraid. Really crazy! – but that's how billions of people *naturally* are.

Another aspect, which we have particularly noted in RET, is that when people become upset about anything, especially when they are quite anxious or depressed, instead of feeling sorry and displeased about their upsetness and working to reduce it, they become enormously upset about their upsetness. They tell themselves, 'I *must* not be anxious, I *must* not be depressed', and then they almost always become much *more* anxious and depressed.

Another problem, stemming from overgeneralizing (which we think, along with Alfred Korzybski (1933) is an innate human predisposition), is that whenever people do quite badly at something important, they easily, but foolishly conclude, 'I am a bad person, I am no good, for doing badly'. Even when they do only one important thing badly, they come to the false conclusion, '*I*, my whole person, am no good', instead of, 'What I *did* is not good'.

People from all over the world seem to do this. For example, in our culture we say 'Because my work is defective, I am a lousy worker and I am no good', while in another society they say, 'Because my hunting is defective, I am a lousy hunter and a lousy person'. Feelings of inadequacy and *self*-downing seem to be rampant among the human race, in every culture. Even though they have different priorities, people denigrate their *selves* for their culturally defined *deficiencies*.

So there is a high degree of probability that humans have an innate tendency to evaluate or measure *acts* (which is good) and also their *essences* (which is inaccurate and often self-defeating). Instead of getting their resources together to change *things* they can change, they whine and scream and yell and horrify themselves by making overgeneralized, global ratings of their *selves*, of other *people*, and of their *whole* environment, and they consequently do less to change their behaviours and environmental conditions than they otherwise could do. So I hypothesize that humans are born *and* raised to think crookedly. Moreover, when people make themselves upset – for example quite anxious – they tend to think *more* crookedly and so they exacerbate instead of ameliorate their emotional problems.

W.D. Now if your hypothesis is correct, that humans are born with a tendency to upset themselves, why do you think that the majority of theories of psychotherapy don't stress this innate tendency amongst humans, but stress the environmental conditions in which they live and were raised as accounting for their disturbance?

A.E. Well, that proves my point, because that's another form of crooked thinking. Just because you do me in, and I immediately feel very angry, I falsely assume that it was your doing me in that made me angry. The human condition is such, that when anything bad happens to you and you quickly respond with a feeling, because your feeling immediately follows the bad happening, you wrongly *perceive* or *conclude* that the event made you upset. Psychologists and psychiatrists and social workers are prone to this same kind of thinking. Because all their lives they have experienced upsetness after experiencing unpleasant events, they connect the two, tend to blame the events, and then they look for reasons, especially in early childhood, why those events upset them. Now they are partly correct, because if we took a hundred children of 3, 4 and 5, and something bad happened to them, they would practically all, according to RET, be crooked thinkers and would say, 'That bad thing made me upset'. And they would also often say, 'Because I did badly about controlling that event, therefore I am a bad person'.

Once you start thinking that way, from the age of 3, 4 or 5 onwards, you tend to take it into everything you do, including psychological 'science'. So practically the entire human race believes that some rotten event, some cataclysm or some devil did them in. They are right pragmatically, because the event frustrated them and balked their desires. But they also think that the event caused their disturbed feelings *about* their healthy feelings of frustration; and they therefore wrongly and self-defeatingly often make themselves panicked, depressed, and enraged.

W.D. Right, but let's take somebody who has been exposed to really noxious environmental conditions over a long period of time – it seems to me from what you are saying there, correct me if I am wrong, that these people have been subjected to two handicaps – firstly the exposure to very negative ongoing life events, which may limit their opportunities to live happily, and secondly an innate handicap, which they may have inherited from their parents.

A.E. You mean the innate handicap of tending to think crookedly about noxious environmental events?

W.D. Right.

A.E. Yes, I would say so. Humans have a great difficulty in keeping *non sequiturs* out of their thinking and most people who are abused by their parents, who are raised in a poverty-stricken family, or who have physical handicaps, will frequently conclude, 'Because this condition is so bad it absolutely *must* not happen; and because it is so bad and has happened over a period of time, it will always *continue*, and it *must* not. If so, that would be *awful*.' Obviously we cannot get rid of noxious stimuli, and these do contribute significantly to human disturbance, because if people only had good stimuli, then maybe they would rarely make themselves depressed and anxious.

The trouble is that people jump to wrong conclusions about noxious stimuli. Incidentally it was a non-therapist, Alfred Korzybski, who very strongly implied that overgeneralizing, *non sequiturs*, and crooked thinking are part of the human condition. Korzybski's main book in 1933 was called *Science and Sanity* and he implied that to become sane, we'd better engage in sane thinking; and he said that when we overgeneralize we render ourselves un-sane – not insane. RET tends to go along with these principles of general semantics.

W.D. OK. Now let's go on to your second major theoretical principle.

A.E. The next principle is the principle of the *Must*. Humans have many irrationalities, but most of these don't get them into serious trouble and they can sometimes live happily with these irrationalities. The main irrationalities that are linked with disturbance and neurosis are absolutist, dogmatic shoulds, oughts, musts, commands and demands, and these can be fairly clearly differentiated from preferences, wishes and desires.

The theory of RET says that if humans would stick to preferences – 'I would like this very much, *but* I don't *have* to have it' – they would not get into so much emotional trouble. But when they take practically any kind of a preference, wish or desire and transmute it into an absolute must – 'Because I like *X* very much I absolutely must have it!' or 'Because I want you to love me, I absolutely must win your love' – they almost always make themselves emotionally disturbed and dysfunctional. There is a very high correlation between their demands, commands, insistences, necessities, and what we call emotional disturbance.

In addition, their unrealistic inferences and some of their illogical overgeneralizations are very frequently derivatives of their absolutistic demands – 'Because I must do very well, and I am not doing as well as I *must* do, it is *awful*, I *can't bear it*, I am *no good*, I will *always* be this way', and so on. When people do make unrealistic, anti-empirical inferences, they tend to do so because of their tacit, unconscious musts. Most of their awfulizing, I-can't-stand-it-itis and self-downing seems to stem from explicit and implicit demands and commands.

W.D. But isn't there an argument that puts it the other way – that in a sense because human beings have a tendency to awfulize, to conclude that they can't stand certain negative experiences then people develop musts?

A.E. Well, that may be so, but RET theory notes that saying about something 'It must not exist' is highly correlated with strong rather than weak dislikes. Very few people say, 'Because I lost at tiddlywinks, it's awful!' But they will say, 'Because I lost the tiddlywinks championship, which I very strongly wanted to win, it's awful!' They very rarely say, 'I can't stand a minor pain in the ass!' But if it's something they *really* hate, then they tell themselves, 'I can't stand it!'

If you ask anybody why such-and-such a bad thing is *awful*, they will usually say, 'Well, because it is very bad.' I would agree that if, say, a member of your family gets killed, that's very bad; or if you lose the best job you ever had, that's very bad. But I would ask, using RET, 'Why is it *awful* that it's bad?' You would probably answer first, 'I really do mean it's very bad, but I am just using different terminology – like it's awful weather, meaning very bad weather.' Second, you would probably admit, or I would soon get you to acknowledge the irrational belief, 'This extreme badness *ought* not to exist, therefore it is awful.' So if you are really saying, 'It's very, very bad, but goddamn it, it should exist, because it does; and no matter how much I dislike it, that's the way it is, tough shit!', you aren't really calling it awful, you're calling it very bad.

W.D. OK, so we have, if you like, two hypotheses. One that says that the musts are primary and that awfulizing evaluations are derivatives from the musts, while the alternative hypothesis puts it the other way round. Could we constuct a research study to test these hypotheses? Do you think that would be possible?

A.E. In theory the answer is yes. A research study on musts would be very difficult, not impossible perhaps, but some good planning would have to be done. I once asked our therapists what we could do to get good empirical evidence for the musts, and the answer was that it is very difficult because most musts are implicit rather than explicit. So if you start giving people questionnaires about their musts, their awfulizing, and their I-can't-stand-it-itis, you are going to have a hard time pinning them down. So theoretically the answer is yes, and actually there have been a few studies which seem to validate or semivalidate the musts. There could be more, but it is going to be a little difficult because of the implicitness of the musts. People often have them and act on them in a self-defeating way, but they often don't bring them to consciousness without good active-directive, probing therapy.

W.D. Now, let's just take your theory about the primacy of the musts. Would you say that RET is mainly a trait theory of disturbance or a state theory of disturbance or both? Let me explain what I mean by that. A state approach would see people as making themselves disturbed in specific situations, but without necessarily having a global tendency to do this, whereas a trait approach would see people as having, if you like, a general tendency to make demands about themselves, others and the world. So in your view is the RET theory of emotional disturbance a trait theory or a state theory, or does it cover both?

A.E. Well, I would say that it is primarily a trait theory because almost all humans have the trait of thinking crookedly and of easily upsetting themselves, and then upsetting themselves about their upsetness. On the other hand it's definitely related to the state, the environment and to situational conditions. Because humans don't just live in a vacuum. You can say they have two main traits – one is their desirousness and the other is their neediness, their 'musturbatory' demands. Humans couldn't live without desire, because they would die if they didn't want to eat and protect themselves. All animals are motivated by desires; and their desire is almost always related significantly to prevailing conditions because those determine how, and whether, it can be fulfilled.

One of the basic ways to fulfil desires is through other people, who can give you love, sex, food, shelter and so on. So conditions, including other people, can be favourable or unfavourable to the fulfilment of desires and therefore desires themselves will fluctuate enormously with the prevailing conditions. Going back to Abe Maslow and his need hierarchy (by which he really meant hierarchy of desires), once you get a primary desire fulfilled, like sex, then temporarily it goes down to the bottom of your list. But then food or something else you desire comes up to the head of your list.

However, your sex drive often has to be fulfilled with some other person, and the availability of food depends on things like its plentifulness and your ability to find or purchase it, so desiring strongly interacts with external conditions. The trait of neediness, on the other hand, is related firstly to the fulfilment of desires – when your sex drive is fulfilled you will be less needy in that respect. But it also tends to have an obsessive-compulsive element, which is independent of desire. You can be needy for love, for example, and never be satisfied, even when you are getting an enormous amount of it. You may tell yourself that even that amount is never enough. You can thereby make yourself into a bottomless pit. So the two aspects, the state and the trait aspects of want and need often go together. But dire neediness can also be independent of state conditions.

W.D. Right, now if we think about the various irrational belief tests that exist in the RET literature, it's possible that people who would upset themselves in certain circumstances – take for example that they may upset themselves when a certain person does not approve of them – may claim not to have an irrational belief about approval if they fill out an irrational belief test when they are *not* upset about being rejected.

A.E. Right, that's why all personality tests tend to be inaccurate. Because people give you some good information and some poor information, because they don't really think their answers through and think differently under different conditions and at different times. Incidentally you would have a hard time answering yes or no to many questions about irrationality because the answer would be yes under certain conditions and no under other situations. 'Yes, I am often needy for ice-cream, but no, I am not often needy for sex.' So unless you ask personality questions carefully, you are often going to get equivocal answers.

W.D. Yes, but a person could say, 'No, I am not needy for ice-cream', because just then they aren't, they don't even have a strong desire for ice-cream just then – but later they might disturb themselves when they really want ice-cream and by turning that into a demand in that specific circumstance.

A.E. Yes, so you are saying that many tests of irrationality leave a lot to be desired?

W.D. Right. But in your writings you have repeatedly argued that if a theory can't be tested, it almost falls outside the realm of science. Let me play devil's advocate for a moment – how are we really going to test your hypotheses, if we don't have good methodologies for testing them?

A.E. Well, we had better get improved methodologies. For example, we can put our question more specifically: 'When you are strongly desirous of having a love partner, then do you need that partner to love you?' But if we ask a general question: 'Are you needy of any partner loving you?', we are not going to get a very precise answer.

W.D. But even if we make that question more specific, I can still imagine that our respondent might say, 'No, I don't need that person to love me', when in fact, in a specific situation when they are faced with the *experience* of not being loved –

A.E. Or when they are faced with it for a long period of time. . . . You see, they might say, 'Oh, I just got out of a love affair, I don't need anybody to love me right now.' But a while later, they may think and feel, 'Oh, I haven't had a love affair for a whole year – or two years or five years. Therefore, I very much *need* it now!' So again, we are showing that tests of irrationality are often not that accurate, and I don't think that I ever said they were.

W.D. Let's suppose that we gave some of the world's leading psychotherapy researchers the task of coming up with good ways of testing some of your hypotheses, and they worked at it, and worked at it, and their conclusion was, 'Unless we come up with an idiosyncratic measure for each client, we can't falsify or validate the theory; and even then, we still can't, because even when we come up with an idiosyncratic measure respondents might only acknowledge their musts when they are actually feeling disturbed at that very moment – and they might not acknowledge their musts even then.' What conclusions would you come to about the scientific status of your theories if indeed it turns out that they really can't be tested?

A.E. I would say, even if we can't directly test the theory itself – like the theory of electricity sometimes can't be tested – then the best thing we can do in psychotherapy is to test the results of the theory. Let's *assume* that the theory is correct, apply it as therapy and then do good studies of the therapy. Then we could test whether the therapeutic application of that theory worked, but we still might not be able to prove the theory itself is true.

W.D. Right, so we can conclude that it is at present very difficult, and perhaps impossible, to come up with good methodologies to test some aspects of RET theory.

A.E. But doesn't that go for any theory? Let's take family systems theory, for example. Much has been written about systems theory. One of its hypotheses seems to be that if you change one member of a family, that changes the family system significantly. Now you can test that aspect of the theory, but maybe you can never test systems theory itself – you can only test its results. And maybe that goes for any psychological theory. Like you can have ten different theories of electricity, none of which you can falsify or validate, but you can still use electricity and see how it works in practice.

W.D. Would it therefore follow that we had better not spend too much time theorizing in RET?

A.E. Or in any form of therapy!

W.D. But even if Rational-Emotive Therapy is an effective therapy in practice, it doesn't mean that the theory which underlies it has been shown to be upheld.

A.E. The same goes for Freudian or any other therapy.

W.D. Let's go on to your third principle.

A.E. The third principle is the principle of force. People strongly hold a philosophy of musts, shoulds, and oughts when they are disturbed and they don't easily give this up. RET says that they don't just have cognitions which upset them, but that to a large degree it's the force – the strength, the dogma, the intensity – with which they hold the cognitions that makes them disturbed. Therefore any effective kind of therapy, such as RET, had better have strong, forceful, dramatic, evocative methods for getting them to give up those musts.

W.D. But isn't dogma by its very definition strong? I mean does it make sense to talk of a 'weak must'?

A.E. Well, let's take a typical one – 'I must be loved by so-and-so'. I hadn't thought about it, but the chances are you could say that weakly or strongly. It would always be a 'warm' cognition rather than a 'cool' cognition, but I think there can be different intensities of even a 'must'.

W.D. Is that what you have found clinically?

A.E Some people admit the must and fairly easily give it up. I just recently had a client who started reading *How to Stubbornly Refuse to Make Yourself Miserable about Anything – Yes, Anything!* (Ellis 1988), and he said that within three weeks of reading it he changed immensely. I believed him, and now I've seen him twice since, and he seems to be doing even better. I am fairly sure that he's got it – meaning that he truly understands and is passionately using RET to help himself. So he had the musts, but he acknowledged them and started giving them up. But I have other clients who see their musts clearly, and even see that they are destructive, but still hold on to them rigidly. So I think there is an emotional variable of intensity which goes with the must. It is pretty clear that you can have mild, moderate or strong desires, so I don't see why you can't have mild, moderate or strong musts.

W.D. How would you test whether people did have mild, moderate or strong musts?

A.E. Well, some of them would acknowledge that they believed in the must e.g. 'I must be loved by so-and-so', and you could ask them: 'Do you mildly, moderately or strongly agree that you must be loved by so-and-so?' That would be one way, though you could question whether they were really being candid. With others you would find out from their behaviour – the rigidity with which they cling to a must. If they knew it was bothering them – and they acknowledged (as some of our clients fairly easily do) that it was screwing them up – and they still didn't give it up, then you could say there was some evidence of strength in their holding it.

W.D. Is there a strong correlation between the degree of conviction in a must and the degree of intensity of the disturbed emotion associated with it?

A.E. Yes, that's another way of saying it. Conviction is a cognitive factor and yet the strength of it seems to be emotive. That's why I would say that cognition, emotion and behaviour are all interrelated. Let's take the people who are devoutly convinced that there was a Jesus, that he was the son of God, and that if they acknowledge him he will give them grace and forgiveness. Now, isn't there, in all probability, a high correlation between their strong convictions and their feelings of achieving grace? In fact, we would have a hard time differentiating between a strong conviction and a strong feeling.

W.D. Now, in therapy one of your major goals is to help people to give up, as far as is humanly possible, any kind of conviction in musts. But, if we can't get them to give up their conviction, in other words if they're just not buying the notion that there are no absolute musts, would it then follow that an alternative strategy would be to help them to go from a very strong belief in their must – for instance, 'I *really* need my husband's love' – to a milder belief in it?

A.E. The answer is probably yes, because the milder conviction can more easily be given up. On the other hand, if they absolutely won't give up the conviction, it might be good to help them acquire another conviction which would let them live more happily. For instance, 'I really *need* my husband's love, but as long as I treat him well, I will surely have it.' This second strong conviction is actually a risky one – because they really can't be sure if they treat their husband well, they will have his love. But as long as they strongly hold this risky conviction, they will not feel anxious or depressed. Or they could 'foolishly' believe, 'I absolutely *must* have my husband's love, but because I pray to a kindly God every night, he will guarantee my having it.' Again, this unrealistic conviction may help them be happy and undisturbed - unless and until reality proves that it is false. That's what a great deal of therapy does – provides clients with dubious, but still strong, convictions that allow them to live, at least for a while, with their foolish musturbatory convictions.

Did I ever tell you about the amusing thing that Johnson (a psychiatrist at Rockland State Hospital in New York) did many years ago? He wrote an article in *Psychiatric Quarterly*, saying that what happens in Freudian therapy is that you're beset by various demons, and then the Freudians convince you that you really want to have sex with your mother. Well, that's a much worse demon, so you give up your prior demons and obsess about the worse one! Then the analyst convinces you that it's natural and OK to want to fuck your mother – and then you are 'cured'!

W.D. What implication does that have for RET?

A.E. Well, I sometimes have old and rather senile clients whom I can't easily reach, because they are absolutely rigid and they won't give up their self-defeating convictions. So I sometimes use a Pollyanna-ish approach like, 'Oh, this is all going to turn out all right', or 'I'm sure you are going to get over this anxiety' – things like that. I strongly persuade them that my conviction – which I don't believe in myself – is undoubtedly true. Some of them then improve significantly. Now that's a very un-ideal solution, but it may be the only one they'll accept, so I therefore sometimes use it. Look at the millions of people who are utterly convinced that God (or the Devil!) personally is supporting them, and who, with this rather silly conviction, make themselves unanxious.

W.D. Let's move on to your next theoretical principle.

A.E. The next thing is, as we mentioned before, that the philosophy of unconditional musts is often held tacitly, implicitly and unconsciously. Some profound musturbators don't really acknowledge that they have any musts, or else admit them and think they are valid. You can bring their musts to their attention and sometimes they say, 'Sure I think I must be loved by significant people at all times. Of course I must!' Other clients feel very upset about not being loved as they supposedly *have* to be, but they sneak in this *have to* and deny that they have anything but preferences, so their musts exist but are tacit. Other clients say, 'Oh yes, I am telling myself I must succeed', but they don't acknowledge how *strongly*, how *pervasively* they believe that they must. So I think that the origin of disturbance is often unconscious in that people don't *see* what they believe implicitly, how strongly they believe it, and how they disturb themselves with their musts.

W.D. What evidence do you have in favour of that notion?

A.E. Well, one piece of evidence is indirect. When people acknowledge the strength of their dogmatic musts and then vigorously think and act against them in therapy, they often radically change their dysfunctional feelings and behaviours. But it's mainly their vigorous work at disputing their imperatives, not just a passive acknowledgement that they have then, that does the trick. People can say lightly, as I point out humorously in many of my workshops, 'Oh yes, I guess I don't *have* to be loved by so-and-so', but then they add much more strongly, 'But I really *should* be!' Haven't you seen that many times in therapy? It would be nice if we had some experiments to show that people often change 'I *don't have* to do well' into 'But I really *should*!' I don't know of any off-hand, and I think it would be great if some researchers did such studies.

W.D. Let's go on to your next principle.

A.E. The next one is the interaction of cognition, emotion and behaviour, and the interaction of the *ABC*s (where *A* stands for Activating event, *B* for Belief, and *C* for Consequence). These all affect each other, according to RET. Our beliefs profoundly affect how we feel, but our feelings, including our desires, strongly and profoundly affect what we believe. The wish is father to the thought, you see; and we have considerable evidence, mainly clinical, that demonstrates this. When you strongly desire to do well, you think in a certain prejudiced way about it – and often you make up rationalizations or excuses when you don't perform well. Suppose you fail at something when you strongly wanted to succeed, aren't you likely to rationalize about your failing?

W.D. And presumably you rationalize even more when you have a must about it?

A.E. Yes, quite so. Similarly behaviour interacts with both emotion and cognition. We know, for example, that often the best way to get rid of an obsessive fear is to force yourself to act against it and to do what you're irrationally afraid of doing. Many people never give up their phobias until they act against them in real-life situations many times. So RET theory has said, from the time I gave my first paper on it at the American Psychological Association in Chicago in 1956, that cognitions, feelings and behaviours interact and are really not separate processes. We seldom have such a thing as a pure feeling, or a pure thought, or a pure behaviour. Cognitive-behavioural therapists are coming around to this idea of interrelatedness now – more than they used to. But they forget that I said this originally in 1956 – that cognition, emotion and behaviour are normally bonded together and in some important respects are interrelated processes.

Similarly RET says that the *A*s, *B*s and *C*s are practically never pure. *A*, the Activating event, really never exists by itself, because you always have some perception or cognition mixed up in it. So *A* is not actually what occurs, but how you *perceive* it occurring. You invariably bring your desires, your perceptions and your previous biases to the Activating event. RET, like systems theory, shows that the relationship between *A*s, *B*s and *C*s are all interactional and systematic. With couples, for instance, the anger of one mate is the Consequence (*C*) of what he or she believes (*B*) about the Activating Event (*A*) that the other mate sets in motion. Then, reacting with Belief (*B*) to this *A*, the second mate may bring about depressed Consequences (*C*), and then his or her Consequence (depression) becomes an Activating event for the first mate to react to with his or her own Belief (*B*) system.

W.D. Let's go on to your next principle.

A.E. The next one is that by and large humans are constructivists, as George Kelly (1955) was the first major therapist to point out. They construct their *A*s, *B*s and *C*s, because they have a biological tendency to do so. Even in early childhood you construct what happens to you, and then later you reconstruct it and re-invent your early childhood. That's why psychoanalysis is so misleading because what you are talking about now is your present reconstruction of what happened then.

The psychoanalysts say that you were given your Belief system by your parents and by your culture – RET says that you largely constructed it, particularly your musts about the fulfilment of your desires. RET holds that you take over many of your standards, goals, values and preferences from others, but even then *you* take them over, and, being a unique individual, you have some *choice* in what standards you accept and how you carry them out. For biological and social reasons, you partly construct your preferences; and then you frequently construct musts about these preferences. So you are a constructivist in relation to your *B*s, your Beliefs. And your emotions and behaviours are also constructed and reconstructed, and are largely correlated with and intrinsically interact with your Beliefs.

I forgot what Kelly said about early childhood, but I suspect he would say you were *given* a lot of your beliefs by your parents and culture. That's what practically all therapies say, except RET. We say that even young children *reconstruct* and *redefine* most of the beliefs they originally are taught during their childhood. They are largely reactors during their first year or two, but after that they increasingly become constructivists.

W.D. It seems to me that while quite a few of the other approaches within the cognitive-behavioural tradition claim allegiance to social learning theory, what you are now saying is really not within the same theoretical system as social learning theory.

A.E. Yes, it is rather different, because RET is perhaps the only therapy and the only major personality theory that clearly distinguishes between the standards, goals and values which people largely learn and their irrational Beliefs about these standards which they largely invent or construct. Kelly hinted that this is so, but wasn't too clear about it. So RET has a different emphasis on ideological self-construction than both the behaviourists who emphasize environmental conditions and the social learning theorists and the psychoanalysts, who emphasize environmental indoctrination. RET holds that our social milieu importantly affects our desires and preferences (because young children are born gullible or teachable) but that we ourselves largely construct disturbing imperatives and absolutist musts about our desires.

W.D. Let's look at your next principle.

A.E. That's concerned with upsetness, which is one of the things that people construct. When they get upset about anything, they know it's not good to be upset and so they put in a must and say, 'I must not be upset, I must not be anxious, I must not be depressed!' instead of, 'I wish to hell I weren't disturbed! Now what can I do about it?' So they exacerbate their disturbances by insisting that it *must* not exist. They are often *more* disturbed about their anxiety and depression than they are about the original failure or rejection that they made themselves upset about. Moreover, as I previously noted, once they bring on a primary or a secondary feeling of great upsetness, that feeling itself helps them think even more crookedly.

W.D. So, since people are rarely taught to upset themselves about their upsetness, and it would be difficult for them to observe other people doing this, you're saying it's mainly a construction?

A.E. Yes, I am. They may, to some degree, hear their mothers and fathers saying, 'I must not be anxious! I must not be depressed!', and their parents may actually tell them, 'You must not be anxious'. But most of the time their feelings of anxiety and depression are internal, so that other people don't observe these feelings and don't tell them that they must not have them. On the contrary, they themselves naturally feel so uncomfortable when they are anxious and depressed that, first, they strongly *desire* to remove their discomfort; and second, they frequently construct a *demand* that they not feel anxious or depressed.

W.D. OK, let's look at your next principle.

A.E. In our approach to psychotherapy we take an unusual view, because we try to be quite scientific. Freud mentioned science continually and thought he was very scientific, but I think he often overgeneralized and refused to look at data that disconfirmed his hypotheses, so that he was frequently anti-scientific. Some therapies, like behaviour therapy, try to be scientific, but many of them, like Gestalt therapy, make little effort to falsify their theories, to change them, and to incorporate scientific methods in the techniques they employ. In RET, we hypothesize that anti-science, dogma, absolutism, or what is sometimes called scientism, is one of the main essences of neuroticism and self-defeating behaviour. Science has three main aspects: one is empiricism or realism – that theories be sceptically checked against empirical data and, when falsified, be changed or abandoned. Second, science uses logic and, often, mathematics to disprove or partially validate its theories. It is sceptical that two contradictory theories are equally viable and useful. Third, science is open, flexible, non-dogmatic and non-absolutist. It does not claim that any theory of people and things absolutely does, and must, hold true under all conditions all the time. Scientific theories – including science itself – are always open to revision and change.

W.D. Ideally!

A.E. Yes, ideally. Individual scientists – like Lysenko – may be rigid and dogmatic. They may, of course, inflexibly stick to a theory, just because it is their theory. George Kelly was the one who said that humans are all scientists because we predict things in advance and then we check our predictions. That was a good insight on his part. But he forgot to say that people are, often, rotten scientists! If they were good scientists they would be more realistic and empirical, they would try to falsify their hypotheses, they would question their contradictory views, and above all they would not be dogmatic. But, being only partially scientific, they often think and behave otherwise.

RET, unlike other therapies, holds that inflexible dogmas, especially absolutist *musts*, which people often construct and foolishly tack on to their legitimate desires, are opposed to a flexible, scientific outlook. So not only do we use the scientific method to check RET theories and practices, but also RETers partially identify with the philosophy of science. I personally favour Karl Popper's comprehensive realism or critical rationality, but I am not contending that it is the final say-so in science. I also am personally opposed to what I call religiosity – or dogma of any kind, including dogmatic atheism – for example, the kind they used to have in the Soviet Union – so the problem isn't just theological religiosity but secular religiosity, devoutness or piousness of any kind. On the contrary, RET espouses an open society, where there are many alternative choices and no dogmas.

W.D. What is your next theoretical principle?

A.E. RET is largely concerned with what people are doing right now to make themselves disturbed – in other words, how they perpetuate their disturbance rather than how they acquired it. Whatever the origin of my disturbance is, if I am upset today I am still thinking nuttily and behaving foolishly, and therefore the goal is to zero in on what I am *now* doing to recreate and to perpetuate my self-defeatism. When RET explores people's past – which it may do briefly – it tries to show them that in this past, including their early childhood, they were upsetting themselves by thinking crookedly, and they are still perpetuating that today. We are mainly interested in people's current dysfunctional thinking and behaviour, more than in understanding the gory details of what happened to them in the past.

W.D. What is your next theoretical principle?

A.E. The difference between self-acceptance and self-esteem. RET says that self-esteem is a measurement and that *any* measurement of the self, even a good measurement, is inaccurate, because self-raters are really saying, 'I am a good person *because* I do good things and am lovable.' We try to get people to give up all self-*rating* in favour of self-*acceptance*, which means, 'I don't rate my *self*, my *being*, or my *essence* at all – only my traits, deeds and acts. I accept myself because I *choose* to do so – *whether or not* I do well, *whether or not* people love me.' That's quite different from self-esteem, which only works temporarily. Because people only tend to esteem themselves while they do well – and even then they are usually anxious that they will do poorly next time! In RET, your self-acceptance is never conditional – you accept yourself however badly you behave.

W.D. Whereas if you esteem yourself, you can always *dis*esteem yourself?

A.E. Right. When you esteem your *self* you really mean, 'I am OK *because* I do well.' Then you are almost forced to say, 'I am *not* OK, I am no good when I do poorly.' But, you see, you can accept yourself *unconditionally*, just because you choose to do so, just because you are alive. Self-acceptance doesn't imply *any* kind of measurement of your self, your being, at all.

W.D. What is your last theoretical principle?

A.E. The last principle is that two main sources of just about all neurosis are, first, ego anxiety or self-downing, and second, discomfort anxiety, discomfort depression, or refusal to accept uncomfortable things in one's life. This is also known as low frustration tolerance (LFT). When humans are quite disturbed they frequently have both of these: they put themselves down for doing the wrong thing or for being unlovable, and then they also believe, 'It's horrible to fail because I am not going to get what I want and *need*!' or 'It's horrible not to be loved because I am not going to be cared for as I *must* be!' These two elements of self-disturbance interact with each other. For example, when you have ego depression or ego anxiety you put yourself down for failing and you make yourself feel depressed and anxious. Then you tell yourself, 'My depression is *too* uncomfortable! I *shouldn't* be that uncomfortable!' So you then create low frustration tolerance or discomfort anxiety about your ego anxiety. Whenever we see a disturbed person in RET we look for evidence of both these things and the important interaction between the two.

W.D. In your experience, working clinically, are there particular major ways in which people put themselves down?

A.E. Yes, the most serious self-denigrators really do consider themselves to be utterly worthless – or, as one of my clients graphically said many years ago, 'I am not just a piece of shit! I am a pimple on a piece of shit!' When they don't do that they have various other kinds or degrees of self-downing, such as, 'I am a lesser person 'or 'I am largely, though not completely, inadequate' or 'Because I am not competent or lovable enough, I am undeserving of real happiness.'

W.D. Or they put themselves down by saying. 'I am evil.'

A.E. That's a bit different. The two main forms of self-downing are, first, feelings of shame or incompetency: 'What will people think of me for being a schmuck, for acting poorly or inadequately, as I must not act?' Second, feelings of guilt or sinfulness: 'I did a rotten, evil act, which I absolutely must not do. Therefore, I am no damned good for being immoral.' In both instances, people tend to believe, 'I am no good.' But incompetence no-goodness and immorality no-goodness are different, and some people bring on both varieties of self-flagellation. Most people, though, mainly feel incompetent and inadequate, because they haven't done that many evil acts. Though I have seen self-deprecators who say, 'I have too much money and other people have less money, and that's evil and immoral and therefore I'm no good.' But the vast majority of people in our culture put themselves down for incompetency, inadequacy, and slobhood rather than for evilness.

W.D. Now, when you talk about discomfort disturbance, you have said that it's often called low frustration tolerance. Are the two concepts really synonymous or do they differ?

A.E. I see them as synonymous. When I first talked about discomfort anxiety I realized that certain forms of anxiety come from viewing discomfort or frustration as intolerable, as against ego anxiety, where one views failure to rate oneself as a great achieving person as intolerable. But I then realized, as other people pointed out to me, that I really meant not just discomfort anxiety, but discomfort disturbance (including discomfort depression and rage) – and that is synonymous with LFT, low frustration tolerance.

W.D. Are there various categories of low frustration tolerance?

A.E. There are two major ones. One is, 'I must have immediate gratification right now!', which one of my current clients has, for example. He must have ice-cream or pizza or whatever food he feels like having at the moment, which is self-defeating because he is very overweight. And then he also has the other form of LFT, which some people don't have, which says, 'I absolutely must not have immediate pain! I can't tolerate doing work, doing homework for therapy, or doing anything really uncomfortable.' So some people believe, 'I must have comfort!' and others believe, 'I must not have any real discomfort!', and many people believe both.

W.D. Now, I have often heard you talk about self-pity as a form of low frustration tolerance. Where does it fit in with the two major types of low frustration tolerance that you've just mentioned?

A.E. Well, if you don't have enough goodies – enough ice-cream, or enough love – you self-pityingly say, 'Poor me!' And if you have what you consider *too much* discomfort, pain or injustice you may also conclude, 'Poor me! Isn't it awful for a nice person like me to be unjustly put upon!' So both types of low frustration tolerance can result in self-pity.

W.D. And where does the concept of deservingness come in?

A.E. Deservingness leads to someone concluding, 'Just because I want it, I absolutely *deserve*, and *should* have, fairness, justice, and comfort, and you bastards aren't giving it to me as you *must*. Therefore, it's not only unfair but absolutely *horrible* and *terrible*, and I *can't stand* being deprived! So I *deserve* goodies – more money, more ice-cream, more sex – and I *deserve* lack of pain and handicaps; and if the world doesn't give me what I deserve, it is a rotten place and I might as well complain like hell and finally kill myself!'

2 MAJOR PRACTICAL PRINCIPLES

WINDY DRYDEN In this interview we'll cover the major practical principles of what good and effective therapy is from your perspective, so let's start off with your first practical principle.

ALBERT ELLIS According to the theory of RET, people largely – though not completely – make themselves inappropriately miserable through their belief systems (their *B*s, in our terminology) – their musts, shoulds, oughts, demands and commands. Because they are mainly responsible for *constructing* their disturbances, they can almost always – if they are neurotic rather than borderline, psychotic, or organically aberrated – choose to *not* disturb themselves and/or to quickly overcome their dysfunctional thoughts, feelings and behaviours. An effective therapist, consequently, can show almost any neurotic, as well as many *more* seriously self-defeating individuals, how to stop making himself or herself miserable. This skill can be especially taught through the process of RET.

W.D. Do you hold any truck with the notion that in some way people are motivated to feel miserable and therefore are reluctant to give up their misery because it is familiar – in a way it helps them to predict the world and therefore they have grown used to it?

A.E. I think that some people do derive secondary gains, as they are called, from their neurosis, from their disturbance. And therefore they are reluctant to give it up. I don't think that they often deliberately hold on to their self-sabotage, except in unusual cases – where, for example, they are getting workman's compensation for being ill. But I do think it is very easy for them to hang on to self-defeating behaviour, because they largely created it in the first place; it is often hard for them to give it up. So the main secondary gain they get from neurosis is *ease* – the *ease* of retaining it and of not consistently pushing themselves to surrender it. But I don't think they actually like the *results* of their disturbance, except in a few instances, and that they therefore *willfully* hang on to it.

W.D. What is your next practical principle?

A.E. That the therapist can show the client that, implicitly or overtly, he or she has various dogmatic ideas, absolutistic demands and insistences – *musts*, *shoulds* and *commands*. These can be revealed to clients fairly easily. And some – though hardly all – people can be induced – persuaded – to quickly start working to give them up and change them back to undemanding desires and preferences.

W.D. How much of a prerequisite is that for effective RET? Can people be helped if they go on claiming that they can't recognize any absolutistic demands in themselves?

A.E. Well, in RET and other forms of cognitive-behavioural therapy the elegant solution – which I think is most likely to reduce present as well as prevent future problems – is to recognize the absolutistic demands and really give them up. But the inelegant solution is frequently to help the client to give up the *derivatives* of their demands, such as, 'Because I *must* have success and because I am not doing well, it is awful that I am not! I can't stand failing! I am no damn good when I do poorly! And I will always fail because I have failed so far!'

Now, if clients just give up the derivatives of their musts they sometimes get close to implicitly undermining the musts themselves, and that can definitely help. But they can surrender their derivative attributions *without* really giving up their underlying musts. So if they *only* dispute these derivative inferences, they achieve an inelegant, that is not too philosophic, solution to their basic demandingness.

Clients can also be helped in many other inelegant ways – such as believing that their therapist likes them. They can get hundreds of inelegant solutions to their problems through therapy. But, as I said back in 1972, most therapy helps people to *feel* better rather than to *get* better. To *get* better they had, first, better give up their musts and, second, also tackle the major (explicit and implicit) inferences and attributions that they derive from these musts (Ellis 1972b).

W.D. What is your next principle?

A.E. That clients had better fight their musts *actively*. They preferably should work hard at fighting them, because the one thing that a hundred years of therapy have mainly shown us is that *insight is not enough*. Even RET insight, which I think is more efficient than other forms of therapeutic insight, is not enough. So the therapist had better teach the client to actively, actively, actively keep persisting at fighting those musts.

W.D. What do you mean by fighting the musts?

A.E. Detecting them, debating them, disputing them, differentiating them from preferences, and returning to preferences in place of the musts. It is especially important to challenge them and their derivatives by asking scientific questions, such as, 'Where is it written that I *must* do well?' 'Prove that it is *awful* to be unloved.' 'Why am I no damn good as a person when I behave badly?' 'How does it follow that because I've failed many times, I will always fail in the future?' People can dispute their irrational beliefs scientifically, in the same way they can dispute scientifically any other hypothesis. And heuristically, they can simultaneously show themselves that unless they rip up their own irrationalities, as well as forcefully *act* against them, they will just go on suffering – and suffering!

W.D. Do you find that quite a few of your clients, when they are debating or disputing their musts, do it in rote or parrot fashion and don't really involve themselves in dealing with the meaning? They seem to be just changing the words around.

A.E. Yes, both the less intelligent clients and the lazy clients do this – the brighter hard-working clients do it much less. It is easy for humans to parrot the right idea. They skip straight from their irrational belief to giving an immediate 'right' answer without doing the disputing in between. You ask them to dispute the belief, 'I *have to* do well,' and they don't ask, '*Why* do I have to?' Instead, they skip immediately to, 'I don't *have to* do well, it would only be unfortunate if I didn't.' It would be better if they actively asked the question, 'Why?' So when they say, .'Yes, I don't have to do well, it would only be unfortunate if I didn't', they then don't parrot that answer and learn to think it through.

W.D. Let's take the process of thinking things through, because it seems to be important. What does thinking through from the clients' perspective involve – what steps would you like to see clients take in order to think things through for themselves?

A.E. Well, clients had better not give an immediate answer – 'I don't have to do well, it wouldn't be the end of the world if I didn't – but work out the proof of that answer as you do in math. To ask, for example, '*Why* don't I have to do well?' or '*Why* wouldn't it be the end of the world?' Then they would tend to end up with answers like, 'I could still be a happy human even if I did this thing badly', or, 'I could still get another job even though I failed at fourteen jobs'. So they preferably should not only state the right answer, but go back and show why the right answer *is* the right answer.

W.D. Do you find that the majority of your clients have difficulty doing that?

A.E. Yes. They do it correctly at times, but they often are sloppy and accept too readily the parroted right answer, as if they really believed it.

W.D. What do you do under these circumstances?

A.E. Well, they come to me and say, 'I'm doing the right kind of disputing but my life isn't changing.' So I say to them, 'Let's see what you are doing', and frequently I can show them just how they are parroting.

W.D. Do you ever play devil's advocate and defend the irrational part of your client to test out in the session to what extent they really have thought things through and can maintain their rational thinking?

A.E. Yes, one of our forceful, vigorous, emotive techniques of RET is to uphold clients' own irrational ideas and try to get them to talk me out of these ideas. That can sometimes show them that they are just parroting a rational idea.

W.D. One of the things that strikes me about our education system is that in a sense we don't encourage people to think for themselves, but rather to take other people's ideas and put them down on paper. I certainly find this with undergraduates. A lot of them have a tough time coming up with their own heart-felt ideas. They can summarize other people's ideas, but find it hard to think for themselves.

A.E. Yes, and there is a new movement in education where teachers do try to teach children really to think for themselves – to do the process of good thinking, and not just arrive at some good results. I think that most fairly bright people *can* do it, but they are lazy and *don't* do it. They come up with the easiest, fastest answer, even though it is a sloppy one.

W.D. What is your next principle?

A.E. That the essential thing for clients to do to change themselves is work and practise. It's easy for people to say to themselves, 'Because I *want* to succeed I *have* to.' But in order to give up their musturbatory thinking, they'd better work very hard and practise very much, against it. So one of the main therapeutic principles of RET is that there is very rarely any way except work and practise, work and practise to help people change.

W.D. How much of that work involves repetition?

A.E. Not mindless repetition, which would be parroting again, but the repetition of thinking things through and vigorously challenging their irrational beliefs over and over again until they really *understand* how self-defeating they are and *see* that they won't work.

W.D. Is there any research evidence in RET which shows that clients who work and practise gain more from the process?

A.E. No, very little controlled research that I know about, but I find fairly consistently that my actively *working* clients can make remarkable changes in a relatively short length of time, whereas I have just as bright and educated clients who don't work and practise – who won't fill out our forms, won't do the homework sheets, won't do the reading, won't bring me new things that bother them during the week – and they generally take much longer to improve.

W.D. And do you also find that clients who are creative and innovative do better than clients who are equally hard-working but who go over the same things in a repetitious manner?

A.E. Yes. I can't prove that as yet with experimental data, but that's my clinical impression. People who are creative and figure out new ways of disputing and acting against their irrationalities definitely do better than those who are uncreative and routine in their disputing.

W.D. How frequently do you find that RET therapists really encourage their clients (a) to work and practise, and (b) to do it in an innovative manner?

A.E. Well, our therapists here at the Institute for Rational-Emotive Therapy in New York, who have been here for a year or two, do it fairly well – not all the time, but fairly often. They are creative and they often encourage their clients to be creative.

W.D. And would you say that you are pretty good on that score yourself?

A.E. I think that I try to be creative, I try to show my clients how to be creative and I encourage them to experiment and try new things. But even I may neglect that aspect to some degree.

W.D. What is your next principle?

A.E. The next principle is to force yourself to do what you are afraid of doing – to take concerted action against your irrational beliefs. If you believe, for example, 'I must not be rejected', and you thereby make yourself anxious about possible rejection, the thing to do is to risk rejection over and over again. You had better keep doing what you are afraid to do, to prove to yourself that when you fail, which you often will, it's not horrible, it's not awful, it's not the end of the world, it's just a pain in the ass. What's more, you often learn by your taking this risk and you get better and better at *not* getting rejected. This process, called *in vivo* desensitization, is one of the main aspects of RET, and I encourage my clients (although I don't always succeed) to do it implosively and frequently – not gradually, as most behaviour therapists recommend. I try to get my clients to talk to ten or twenty new people a week, rather than merely one if they are afraid of rejection. Or if they are afraid of elevators, I encourage them to go in twenty elevators a day rather than one every twenty days. I find that those who are willing to act against their phobias implosively overcome them much more quickly, and as far as I can see much more thoroughly. By taking antiphobic *action* they really give up their irrational *ideas* about the 'horror' of the things they are afraid to do.

W.D. So your firstline strategy is to encourage them to practise *in vivo*, presumably both through action and through simultaneous disputing of their irrational beliefs, and preferably to do this implosively. What happens when clients steadfastly refuse to confront their fears intensively?

A.E. Then I will try to get them to do it gradually, or perhaps with a confederate. For instance, they may do something they are phobic about – such as riding in the subway – with a friend of theirs. Or go in a feared elevator with a friend or relative, or sometimes with an assistant therapist.

W.D. It seems that there are some emotions like guilt which it's difficult to take action against, because it would be unethical for a therapist to ask a client to break their moral code so that they could practise accepting themselves while they were doing it! Do you find that where it's easier for clients to take action against their emotional problems, they make more progress than in cases like guilt where taking action is more problematic?

A.E. Yes, I would say so. Though sometimes I can get people to take action against guilt. For example, a daughter thinks that she must see her mother much more than she wants to and is guilty if she doesn't, so I encourage her to see her mother less. Or I may have a client who hates living with his family, but he guiltily won't leave them. So I may show him that if he does take the risk of separating from them, he can more easily get over his guilt than if he stays with them. So it is possible, but much more difficult, to overcome guilt feelings by acting against them. But usually activity assignments work better with phobias rather than with guilt.

W.D. Right, now what is your view of implosive imagery methods?

A.E. Well, I have used them at times – for instance Stampfl's method with snake-phobics, where he gets people to visualize the snakes writhing around their hands and thereby helps desensitize them to snake phobias. But more often I use rational-emotive imagery where I get people to envisage the very worst thing that could happen to them, to feel very upset, to strongly get in touch with their disturbed feelings, and then to make themselves feel appropriately sorry and displeased rather than inappropriately anxious, depressed and enraged. The trouble with Stampfl's method is that it has been found that some people actually get worse with it. They start visualizing the snakes curling around their hands and then they get more phobic than ever. While if you use rational-emotive imagery and induce them to visualize the snakes and then to make themselves feel very concerned and displeased rather than horrified about their images, that enables them to overcome their phobias.

W.D. What is your next principle?

A.E. To welcome the discomfort of certain situations, like a rotten boss or a bad marriage, and not to cop out of it till you get rid of your horror, rage, and low frustration tolerance about it. To stay in the uncomfortable situation, including the discomfort of therapy, while getting rid of your disturbance – and then maybe leave the boss or leave the marriage or leave whatever you dislike. I see hundreds of people every year who are angry at their wife or husband, or enraged at their boss, and who want to quit their job or their marriage. But I encourage them to stay in this obnoxious situation and really work on their rage, so that they replace it with appropriate feelings of frustration and disappointment. Then later they may even see that the annoying job or marriage also has distinct advantages and therefore decide not to leave!

Then there is another technique, that is very popular among cognitive-behavioural therapists, and that I started to use in the late 1950s: that is to encourage clients to write down *E*, their Effective new philosophy which they arrive at by Disputing (at point *D*) their irrational Beliefs (*B*s). Using *E*, they compose a list of coping statements, write down on 3 × 5 cards, and carry around with them so that they can vigorously change their irrational beliefs. They can dispute, 'Why do I need what I want?' and then answer very strongly, 'I damn well *don't* need it, no matter *how much* I want it! If I don't get it, *tough*! – but never *awful*!' Then they powerfully repeat to themselves, and *think* about, these coping statements many times.

They can also tape record an irrational idea – 'I must have so-and-so love me! I'll die if s/he doesn't!' They then vigorously dispute it on tape and bring the tape into therapy; and I listen not only to how accurately but also how *vigorously* they do their disputing.

I also created, in the late 1960s, my famous shame-attacking exercise, which is very emotive and evocative. Using this exercise, clients go out in public and do something foolish, ridiculous or shameful, risk being scorned or laughed at, and vigorously talk to themselves so that they *don't* feel embarrassed, humiliated or ashamed.

W.D. Are these exercises more accurately termed embarrassment-attacking exercises, because it seems to me that one of the differences between shame and embarrassment is that you are more likely to feel ashamed when you reveal something very inadequate, whereas embarrassment is less serious?

A.E. I hadn't thought about that – you may be right that Embarrassment often means a light kind of shame. But in America we frequently use 'shame' and 'humiliation' as a synonym for embarrassment. But they could be called embarrassment-attacking exercises. It all depends on the individual who performs them. For example if somebody gets up in a group of a thousand people and deliberately asks a stupid question and is laughed at by the audience, he or she would often feel very ashamed rather than just lightly embarrassed.

W.D. Let's take that example, because one of the cognitive dimensions which seems to be involved in different emotional experiences is that of intentionality. Now I would certainly agree that if a person stood up and *un*intentionally said something stupid he or she would feel ashamed, but when you do it intentionally, aren't you in a sense saying that it's not really me – I would be inadequate if it was unintentional but since I am doing it deliberately it's not so bad?

A.E. Yes, that's true, though if the people in the audience really put you down, if they really laughed uproariously and thought you were a fool when you intentionally said something stupid, then you would tend to feel quite ashamed. That is what people who deliberately do my shame-attacking exercises usually report. But I agree that most of the exercises my clients actually do are more embarrassing than shameful. Occasionally they do risk real shame. For example they may be very lousy at public speaking and they deliberately go and give a speech, where they don't deliberately stutter or stammer, but still are anxious and therefore speak badly. They then feel real shame. But most of the time they do what you would call embarrassment-attacking exercises. All the same, they often achieve profound results. Because normally they would never deliberately risk doing something embarrassing. Sometimes they take several weeks to force themselves to do it. In my regular therapy groups, every year I give all the members this exercise; and only after two or three weeks of procrastinating will several group members yell out the stops in the subway, or beg, or wear an outlandish outfit, or some other embarrassment-attacking exercise. So it depends on the person. Some of the group members never do it, because they feel so ashamed. But the majority who do the exercise almost always benefit from doing it and thereby surrender some of their dire need for others' approval.

W.D. What is your next principle?

A.E. The next one would be humour. In RET we think that people hold on to their nutty ideas with a lack of humour, and if they're attacked – the ideas, not the people – in a humorous fashion, then sometimes they will see how funny and ridiculous their ideas are and tend to give them up. We give everybody here at the Institute a sheet of my rational humorous songs which they can sing to themselves. So sometimes when they feel depressed they can sing an anti-depression song, or if they feel anxious they can sing an anti-anxiety song. Some people really benefit from these kinds of things and the more we can get them to have a sense of humour about some of the things they take too seriously, the less likely they are to keep taking them overseriously.

W.D. Do you find that clients vary a lot on how they respond to therapist's humour?

A.E. Yes, very much so, because some really take it very well, but some don't. We sometimes get a therapy group to comment, in my absence, on how I conduct the group, and they often mention that the thing they get most out of it is my sense of humour. Because I frequently make humorous cracks, that dispute some of the member's unhumorous irrational Beliefs. For others, humour doesn't mean anything, and still others even get upset about it and take it amiss. So it never works with all clients, and it obviously includes some dangers. Educationally, in courses and workshops, I find that my rational humorous songs almost always go over very well and are therefore useful to a number of the course or workshop members.

W.D. What is the next principle?

A.E. That real vital, absorbing interest in something can be very helpful. People who get vitally absorbed, even in crazy pursuits – such as a devout religious cult – can temporarily, or sometimes even permanently if they remain devout, get distracted from their anxiety, their depression, their horror, or their rage. If they can find something big and ongoing, like devoting themselves for a good many years to a cause, a family, or building a business, they may not really change their irrational philosophy that much, but they get deflected from their disturbance and can live much happier lives. For instance, my clients with an obsessive-compulsive disorder (OCD) have a biological and psychological tendency that drives them to very easily obsess, obsess and obsess. So if I help them to become absorbed in a constructive obsession, like helping people or something like that, they find this much better than the destructive and silly obsessions they otherwise have. So a real vital ongoing interest can help many people to overcome their disturbance or at least to live more happily in spite of it.

W.D. Do you find that people vary in how much absorption or involvement they can summon up?

A.E. Well, they do vary in how much they get involved; but I would say that most really disturbed people are so involved in their disturbance that they would often benefit from getting quite involved with something else, and some of them do. A good example is AA (Alcoholics Anonymous). Almost all alcoholics are disturbed people to begin with, as far as I have found. Then they drink to 'drown' their pain and have a hard time giving it up and facing and working to surrender their anxiety and depression. Millions of them join AA and get over their drinking, and a good percentage of these get utterly devoted to AA. Even though they are often nutty and devout about AA itself, they may thereby acquire a better mode of disturbance than they had before they drove themselves into alcoholism.

W.D. Do you find your clients frequently get vitally absorbed or obsessed with RET?

A.E. Yes, some of them do, and for some of them it's a very good thing. They come around to my Friday Night Workshops for a long time, some of them for years. They get very involved in RET and proselytize to their friends about it; and sometimes they help themselves considerably. They are so absorbed in RET that they use it to talk their friends out of some of their own irrational ideas; and they even send some of them to our Institute for therapy. They read RET books, listen to cassettes, and some of them make RET practically a lifetime devotion in a rather crazy way. I am not sure how much these devout RETers benefit compared to those who are strongly, but not piously, RETish.

W.D. Can RET become a cult?

A.E. No question, it can; and some of the most rigid people use it in a cultish manner and even distort it. They'll take extreme views like, for example, you shouldn't be sad about anything, so let's get rid of all sadness and feelings of frustration. They go to ridiculous extremes and thus bastardize RET. Some of the obsessive-compulsives actually become obsessed with RET. Though this is usually less harmful than their other obsessions and compulsions, it would be better if they didn't take anything, including RET, to such extremes. People can get devoutly absorbed in any form of therapy, not only RET. My observation is that they do so much more with some of the other therapies – such as psychoanalysis and Reichian Therapy – than with RET, because these therapies encourage dogma, while RET is sceptical, rational and opposed to devoutness.

W.D. What is your next principle?

A.E. We try to encourage clients to use many different ways to get rid of their misery – to really work at it, to read, to go to our workshops, and to try a variety of other cognitive, emotive and behavioural techniques in addition to our basic method of Disputing irrational Beliefs. RET is practically always multimodal and consequently we would rarely *only* try to talk people out of their irrational ideas.

W.D. Arnold Lazarus would argue that RET was actually trimodal and not multimodal in the sense that he's defined the term. How would you react to that point?

A.E. You could call it that, but trimodal means probably a dozen cognitive methods, another ten emotive methods, and another dozen behavioural methods. If we add these up they would almost always cover his BASIC I.D. Except that the only thing we (and most other therapists) would do less than he would be what he calls the use of sensation – and I don't know if even *he* does it that much.

W.D. He argues in his chapter in 'Inside RET' that rational-emotive therapists use imagery methods sparingly and in a restricted manner (Lazarus 1989).

A.E. Well, that's because most of the imagery methods and most of the sensation methods he personally uses are, in my estimation, highly ineffective. The positive visualization he employs, for example, helps people, some of the time, to *perform* better but also encourages them to think they *have to* do so in order to be self-accepting. Instead, we favour rational-emotive imagery because it helps people to accept themselves unconditionally even when they are performing *badly*.

W.D. In terms of using many methods of change, do you find that clients have a preference for certain types of techniques – that some people might prefer using cognitive methods while others might use them sparingly and go for the more dramatic and forceful emotive methods, and still others might prefer the behavioural methods?

A.E. Oh yes, very definitely. Some people, for example, really like the homework forms and they fill out one or two every week, even after therapy, and other people rarely do it, so that you have to keep after them to fill out a single one. Others like rational-emotive imagery and do it all the time. I just give them the exercise once and tell them to keep using it, and they *do* keep using it, while some clients practically never do it. So clients often concentrate on what they really enjoy doing. So do therapists. I've seen RET therapists who take the idea of rational-emotive imagery and switch it around their own way because they like imagery, and they give lots of imagery assignments and concentrate less on changing the client's beliefs and behaviours.

W.D. Do you encourage your clients to go with the techniques that are within their modality preferences, or do you sometimes encourage them to go against their natural tendencies, to push themselves and use techniques that in a sense aren't natural to them?

A.E. Sometimes I let them do what they like to do. But sometimes they won't do precisely the thing which would help them most, like *in vivo* desensitization. For instance, socially anxious people may do everything *except* go out and talk to members of the other sex. Then I keep after them to do what they don't want to do, or even what they are horrified of doing.

W.D. Let's suppose that we took two groups of RET clients, each of which used a similar number of techniques, would you hypothesize that the group which used techniques across the cognitive, emotive and behavioural modalities would do better than the group which used only cognitive, or only behavioural, or only emotive techniques?

A.E. I would definitely hypothesize that. I could be wrong, because some people might change their cognitions so well that emotive and behavioural methods might almost be a waste of time for them. But my guess is that the clients who used all three of the main modalities of RET would be the ones to get better quicker and more thoroughly and who would maintain their progress.

W.D. What is your next principle?

A.E. To encourage clients to persist at change, to keep pushing them to work and work, not just at the beginning (as they might work at a diet), but to continue to do so, often for the rest of their lives. The theory says that if they persist at changing themselves for a while, if they really work at it, then some of the changes become second nature and automatic, but some of them don't. So the therapist keeps encouraging the client to persist and persist in a forceful manner, and when clients fall back (which they often do) to persevere in overcoming their irrational Beliefs and their dysfunctional feelings and behaviours once again.

W.D. Now in our earlier interview, you distinguished between ego disturbance and discomfort disturbance. Do you have a sense that one or the other kind of disturbance is harder for clients to stay clear of?

A.E. That may depend on the client. For example schizoid individuals with exceptionally low self-acceptance and a strong tendency to down themselves may have a harder time giving up their ego disturbance while the disorganized clients, the procrastinating clients, and the OCD (obsessive-compulsive disorder) clients may have more difficulty giving up their discomfort anxiety and discomfort depression. In general, I find that people who have difficulty in ameliorating their low frustration tolerance are likely not to make much progress and fall back easily, because they bring their LFT problems into therapy, whereas people with ego problems may not greatly bring that problem into therapy.

W.D. Do you recommend that clients practise disputing their irrational Beliefs even when they have made gains and are not upset?

A.E. Yes, I usually encourage them to dispute their irrational Beliefs when their dysfunctional feelings occur, and whenever they act self-defeatingly. And I tell them that it's also desirable to regularly dispute their irrational Beliefs even when they are not disturbed. They can imagine an activating event occurring about which they often upset themselves and practise with that, so they don't have to wait till they actually feel disturbed. Preferably, they should do this a few times a day whether or not they are acting dysfunctionally.

W.D. Do you find that most clients will do this, or only some clients?

A.E. Some will do it, especially using techniques like rational-emotive imagery. But others will rarely do anything unless they are truly upset. On the other hand, many clients tell me that when they are disturbed, that's when they are *least* likely to use RET techniques, because they then more easily indulge in their disturbance!

W.D. I was going to ask you that – clients often report that they find it very difficult to dispute their irrational Beliefs in the heat of their emotional disturbance, particularly with panic or strong feelings of anger.

A.E. Yes, many do. So I show them that it is *difficult* but not *impossible*. When experiencing panic, it may be almost impossible to do effective disputing. If so, they can then use relaxation techniques to calm down and do active Disputing later. But I strongly encourage them to Dispute and to use powerful coping statements, not to give up, even to try to do so during attacks of panic and depression. If they can't do it then, they had better make sure that they do so later and not just indulge in their upsetting feelings.

When they give into anger, for instance, I give them my famous illustration of my own anger. Thus, in doing my regular Friday Night Workshops, where I publicly conduct RET sessions with volunteers from my audience, I tell everybody to shut up now because I am going to conduct the workshop and their neighbours in the audience would rather hear me and the volunteer client rather than their talking. Often, someone starts talking up immediately in the audience, and I look at them and say, 'That means you. Shut up!' Sometimes they still don't quieten down but instead start arguing with me. 'I am not talking, someone else is.' Then I sometimes get angry and tell them, 'Either shut up or go back in the john and masturbate' or 'One more word and we'll throw you the hell out!' Even though I'm quite angry, and not merely displeased, right then and there, and even though I'm still in the midst of conducting a workshop, I am able to say to myself, 'Oh shit, I'm making myself angry. What am I telling myself?' And I answer, 'They *shouldn't* be the way they indubitably are!' And I say to myself, 'But they *should* be! That's the way they are!' Then my anger immediately goes right away, and I quietly go on with the Friday Night Workshop. So I show my clients that it's possible to dispute irrational Beliefs even while they are experiencing strong disruptive emotions.

Another illustration is when my clients are sitting with a group of people and are scared shitless of talking up. I show them then, that because they are doing relatively little, they can actively dispute their irrational Beliefs (IBs) that create their feelings of panic and force themselves to talk up. It is much more difficult to debate and act against IBs when you have a strong than when you have a mild disruptive feeling. But I strongly show my clients that this can be done.

W.D. Would you recommend that clients dispute their irrational Beliefs as soon as they start to experience a dysfunctional emotion rather than waiting until that dysfunctional emotion becomes so powerful and so makes it less likely that they are going to dispute their ideas effectively?

A.E. Yes, I would recommend two things. First, as soon as they start getting anxious or otherwise upset, don't let the anxiety, depression, or the anger overwhelm them. See it as uncomfortable but *not* horrible or deadly. Second, if their panic or rage really seems overwhelming, then they still can do their best to dispute it right then and there. If they do so and they sometimes succeed – as they at least occasionally will – this will dramatically show them they *can* surrender their irrational Beliefs right then and there, or at least fairly soon afterwards. I tell them, 'Don't let your disruptive feelings go on too intensely or too long. Stop it when it's lower, right at the beginning. But even when it gets intense, which it sometimes will, go after it and force yourself to change it to an appropriate negative feeling. Don't give up! Be *determined* to dispute and act against it until you really change it.'

W.D. What's your next principle?

A.E. In RET we encourage people to try to use elegant Disputing, and that means two things. First, to Dispute their unrealistic inferences and attributions. Thus, if they tell themselves, 'I failed at this task, I must have done it poorly, worse than others would do it. And if I did it poorly then I will always do poorly', they are to question whether these self-statements are empirically true. 'Did I *really* do the task poorly and worse than others would do it? And, if I did, does that mean I will *always* do poorly?'

Second, when people do correct empirical Disputing and rationally conclude, 'Even if I failed this task, that doesn't necessarily mean I did it poorly and it certainly doesn't mean that I will always do poorly', RET encourages them to go on to elegant or anti-musturbatory Disputing, to take their Activating events to the worst extremes and *still* not seriously disturb themselves. Thus, they can say to themselves: 'Suppose I *do* always do poorly, *never* get a good job, and even end up on welfare. Why *must* I do well? Why would I be a *totally inadequate person* even if I did?'

Using elegant, anti-musturbatory Disputing, people can even conclude: 'Yes, the aeroplane I am flying on most likely will not crash. But suppose it does and suppose I actually die, where is it written that I *must* not die? Why do I need a *guarantee* that I won't? In what way would my death be *unthinkable* and *absolutely horrible*?' Using RET, we often help people Dispute their ideas about the worst possible thing that could happen. Not only some minor thing, the awfulness of which is easier to Dispute but which still leaves them with the possibility that the worst thing *could* happen and the irrational Belief that *therefore* this thing *must* not occur and would be *completely intolerable* if it did.

W.D. Is the timing of that important? In your writings you make quite clear that one of the distinguishing features of RET is that elegant disputing is the first-line approach – assume the worst and let's help you get over the worst so that you can then much more easily get over things which are far from being the worst. But do you find that that can backfire with clients who may be willing to Dispute elegantly later after you have helped them to deal with the less dire circumstances they upset themselves about, but who can't jump to elegant disputing right away?

A.E. Yes, I find that true at times, but I often find the opposite. When clients do the less elegant Disputing they stick with it and refuse to go on to the more elegant form. Thus, they may feel so good about the idea, 'One of these days I will marry, and therefore it's not awful to be alone', or 'Soon I will get a good job, and therefore, I don't have to have it right now', that they stop right there. They often don't go on to. 'Yes, but suppose I never marry?' or 'Suppose I never get a good job?' So they remain basically anxious. If feasible, RET helps them to see that no matter *what* unfortunate *Activating* Events occur in their lives, they can *still* find some enjoyments and most probably have a decent existence.

W.D. And what guidelines do you use for yourself in distinguishing between whether to go for the elegant form first or whether to wait till later?

A.E. I usually go straight to more elegant disputing, but in some cases where I think it may boomerang I start with clients' unrealistic inferences and Dispute them first. But I almost always go on to Dispute their basic *musts* and other definitional irrational assumptions. It depends on my judgement about the client. But I generally show them how to do both elegant and inelegant Disputing.

W.D. Under what circumstances wouldn't you go for elegant Disputing at once?

A.E. Well, for example with older people who are not going to make – in my estimation – any profound philosophic change. I have one woman who lives in Staten Island and who won't come to Manhattan and walk a few blocks there because she's afraid of falling, though she will walk in Staten Island. I have a hard time inducing her to walk in Manhattan and she often comes up with the idea, 'Well, one of these days I will be able to do it'. I go along with that because I don't think she is going to get to the point of saying, 'Well, suppose I do it and fall. Would *that* be awful?' And every once in a while I interpolate, 'Yes, I am absolutely sure that one of these days you will be able to do it.' Then I add, '*But* if you fall you won't be hurt very much and it won't be the end of the world.' So I get that kind of elegant Disputing in, too. But if she repeats, 'One of these days I will be able to do it', in her particular case I let it go at that, while with a younger person who is likely to do more elegant Disputing, I would try harder to help her get to a more elegant solution.

W.D. What is your next practical principle?

A.E. To look for alternative solutions, which could be both on the philosophic and the practical level. The trouble with people is that they resort to rigid thinking, say there is no solution to their problems, or stoutly hold that all the solutions are awful, terrible and horrible. So they don't look for alternative solutions.

W.D. What kind of alternatives do you mean?

A.E. Well, first let's take the philosophic ones. On the philosophic plane, they find some inelegant solution and they stick with that. Such as, 'One of these days I am going to marry, or get a good job, or succeed at public speaking', or something like that. They refuse to see that these good things may *not* happen and that they can still be a happy human if they never occur. You see, if you have the open-ended, alternative-providing philosophy, you are really saying to yourself that no matter *what* happens – barring being tortured to death slowly or something like that, in which case you might rationally kill yourself – you can find *some* way of accepting it philosophically and still find *some* happiness. Being determined to find alternative roads to happiness when the one you most want is not open is one of the main essences of non-disturbance. In the practical realm, too, disturbed people will only think of one solution. 'I must go to *this* school', or 'I must take *that* course', or 'I must marry this person and *only* this one'. They don't think of alternative practical solutions that sometimes would be very good, and that sometimes wouldn't be *as* good but would still enable them to lead a decent life. So, using RET, a therapist doesn't just show clients a single philosophical solution or one or two practical solutions, but encourages them to believe that in almost all difficult situations there are alternative solutions that wouldn't be too bad.

W.D. So this is what we talked about in our first interview when we spoke of encouraging clients to be flexible.

A.E. That's right. That ties in with the aspect of RET which includes practical problem-solving. You can actually teach people, and at times we do, how to be better problem-solvers – to set suitable goals, to plan how to achieve them, to test out possible solutions, to try new paths if the old ones don't work and so on. We thereby help them to achieve better solutions to their difficulties. But instead of mainly suggesting these solutions ourselves, we try to show them how to arrive at their own answers – how to become self-solvers. We often suggest various alternative ways of solving a problem, and let the clients figure out which would suit them better. We also have collaborative brain-storming sessions with the client, and again encourage them to actively participate – and to prepare themselves for personal problem-solving when they are on their own or with their regular associates.

W.D. So, in terms of sequencing, I guess you would argue that encouraging clients to be philosophically flexible had better be done before encouraging them to be more flexible, practical problem-solvers.

A.E. Right, but sometimes RET practitioners really do both at the same time, because clients come to us with very practical-problems – 'How will I have more money?' or 'Where will I get a place to live?' So from the very first session we might help them give up their philosophic demands and also help them with practical suggestions.

W.D. What is your next practical principle?

A.E. One thing we emphasize is cognitive homework, not just behavioral homework. We have an RET self-help form and we have the technique of Disputing irrational Beliefs (DIBs) and various other techniques where we get clients to think self-helpingly. One form of cognitive homework which I practically always use, for example, is getting clients to monitor what unfortunately happens to them and what they tell themselves when it happens. They look for their musts, shoulds and oughts and then dispute them either in their head or on paper.

Another technique is referenting, where I ask them to take a few days to write down the advantages of, say, giving up smoking and the disadvantages of not giving it up. Another form of cognitive homework is the hedonic calculus, which is used in decision-making and where clients write down, say, all the advantages of buying this car and all the disadvantages of buying it. Then they rate each advantage and disadvantage from one to ten, add up the scores and see what the total is. They compare this total to the total of buying another car or of making a different decision, so in RET we encourage the doing of considerable cognitive homework as well as behavioural and emotive-evocative homework. Another form of cognitive homework consists of coping statements. Clients write down various coping self-statements, and go over them several times a day.

W.D. As you know, Joe Yankura and I have written a book on your practical approach to therapy (Yankura and Dryden 1990) and in listening to your tapes, one of the things we found is that you seem to have a definite penchant for giving cognitive homework rather than behavioural activity homework. Would you agree with that?

A.E. No, there you have a false impression.

W.D. Well, we listened to over a hundred tapes.

A.E. I can tell you why you got a false impression. Very frequently somebody comes in for their first session and says, 'I am not going out with women (or men) and I always avoid meeting them and stay at home instead.' Right away I say, 'What are you telling yourself to make yourself afraid of encountering them?' Then I give them cognitive homework on that and get them to report instances of and to change their irrational Beliefs that stop them from socializing. But I also always tell them, 'Now if you really want to get over this, practically the only way is to force yourself to go out and accept that you will be uncomfortable, but still approach potential partners.' I may not call it a homework assignment – I may not say, 'Your homework this week is to go out and talk to five people' – but I really see it as a homework assignment, and I fairly steadily tell them things like that without labelling my directives as homework.

W.D. Now that's interesting, because I suppose a criticism that could be levelled against you is that if encouraging clients to put their learning into practice is so important in RET, doesn't it follow that maybe it's important to highlight that more, to emphasize it more than you do?

A.E. Well, that may be correct, I may be lax there, and maybe I could be more precise about it. Instead of saying, 'Now look, you'd damn well better start going out and talking to women', I could give them more concrete instructions about doing it. But frequently I don't label a task as homework when it really is homework. One of the reasons I may have got into that habit is that so many people, especially LFT (low frustration tolerance) people, are allergic to anything you call homework. If you say, 'Now look, the way you get over your problem is to do this, and you are not going to get over it until you really bite the bullet and make yourself uncomfortable', that's one thing. But if you say, 'Unless you do your homework, unless you do this five times a day for the next few weeks you are not going to get over this problem', they may well react against it and not do it. So that may be why I originally started approaching activity homework a bit obliquely – but of course I may be wrong. Also, in my group therapy, where I have ten people in each group and can only spend ten or fifteen minutes with each member, we not only give each one a specific homework assignment and write it out on a slip of paper to give to them but we check each week to see if they've done it. Maybe I'd better do something similar with my individual therapy.

W.D. What is your next practical principle?

A.E. One of the things we definitely try to get people to do is to be open about what their problems are, open with themselves and preferably also open with others – to be able to tell others that 'I am an alcoholic' or 'I don't make too much money' and not to down themselves if they get rejected. One of the examples which I fairly frequently give, is that if a male is afraid to go out with women or to go home with women because he might be impotent, I tell him that one of the best things to do is that when he next meets a woman, wants to go home with her, and feels afraid of exposure, to tell her openly that he has a sex problem and that he is likely to be anxious and to fail at first if they go to bed. I encourage my clients, 'Be open with yourself and with others, and as a shame-attacking exercise let others know what some of your problems are. Because if you try to hide a problem you will have to pretend to be what you aren't and only get falsely accepted. If you show your flaws, the right people for you will still accept you as you are. And if you hide your flaws, you'll give yourself no chance to correct them, whereas if you are open about them you achieve much greater intimacy and get the opportunity to change'. So in RET we frequently encourage self-disclosure, both in and outside of therapy.

W.D. What theoretical justification arising from RET theory do you have for doing that?

A.E. Because non-disclosure, secrecy, tends to increase anxiety. When a man with problems of impotence is about to go home with a woman and he has hidden his problems from her, he is saying to himself, 'Will she find out? Wouldn't it be awful if she found out!' But when he tells her that he has a problem – whether it is about sex, work, money, or whatever – he is much freer and less anxious and will probably perform better with her. When performance anxiety is concealed, it usually escalates. When it is faced and discussed, it often diminishes.

W.D. What is your next practical principle?

A.E. The principle of RET with regard to the therapeutic relationship is that you are usually not going to get very far with clients without establishing rapport with them. If they dislike you, they often won't open up nor listen very well. So you'd better establish rapport with them by showing them that you have a real interest in helping them.

Now the problem is that when you do that, they may interpret it as indicating that you like them or love them personally, and RET sees that as a danger because then they can easily seem to do their homework and to feel better for the wrong reasons – to please you. 'Because I like my therapist I will do my homework, but once I am through with therapy I will never do it.' Or 'Because I like my therapist I think he has good ideas, therefore I will follow his ideas.'

The Achilles' heel of this kind of therapy is that clients become dependent; and one of the main principles of RET is to help them become *in*dependent, to think for *themselves* and acquire *self*-helping habits rather than to remain needy of therapeutic succouring. So in RET we aim for a good relationship and good rapport, but we don't necessarily want to create an involved love–hate relationship – transference–schmansference and that kind of therapist–client sickness. Close personal relationships with clients can easily interfere with the process of therapy, or at the very best can induce people to do the right thing for the wrong reasons. Only rarely do they probably help them think more rationally for themselves. RET also encourages clients to accept themselves *un*conditionally. In person-centred therapy you may say to your therapist, 'Because I perform badly, I am no damn good'. Then the therapist responds, 'Well, I really think you're OK, I really like you'. Then you say to yourself, 'Because my therapist likes me, I really *am* OK'. You then have *conditional* self-acceptance. In RET we want you to think you are OK because *you* have decided you're OK, even if your therapist *doesn't* like you.

So in RET we establish a good relationship by helping clients, but also through giving – and *teaching* – them *un*conditional acceptance. The therapist shows clients by both her words and her manner, that she thoroughly accepts them, even if the client acts poorly in his or her life or in the therapy itself – for example, they come late or don't pay their bills. But then, unlike person-centred therapists, we also very clearly tell the client, 'But if you keep acting obnoxiously in therapy and in your outside life you will most likely get bad results and sabotage yourself.' So we are able to criticize the client's *acts* without damning the *client*.

W.D. Do you think that because RET emphasizes so many techniques and technical procedures that there is a danger of the therapist overemphasizing techniques and underemphasizing the importance of developing rapport?

A.E. Certainly that can happen; but on the other hand I think, from listening to many tapes of people doing RET, that most of them, because they didn't begin with RET but by doing some other form of therapy, tend to go to the other extreme and emphasize rapport rather than techniques. If anything, I find that they are being too nice and passive most of the time, though some of them do go to the opposite extreme and overemphasize techniques.

That's another aspect of RET practice: we hold that when the therapist sees what clients do and what they tell themselves, looks below the surface at their basic self-sabotaging philosophies, and shows them how to discover these for themselves and Dispute them, the therapist often thereby achieves fine rapport. For clients then tend to feel unusually understood. Because the RET therapist's understanding is deeper than psychoanalytic or other therapeutic understanding, clients who seek real help tend to appreciate this. They frequently seem to conclude, as several studies of therapy have shown, that the therapist is quite competent, that she knows more than they do, and that she knows what had better be done and how to get the clients to do it. I think that in behaviour therapy the same thing happens. Clients decide, 'My therapist appears to be a competent person and therefore I like her, will listen to her, and try to do what she asks me to do.' So I think that when RET is done well, much rapport comes through client's view of therapists' competence.

W.D. Are you aware of varying the type of rapport that you try to develop with different clients?

A.E. Yes, very definitely. With most clients I have a rapport based on my being authoritative, but not authoritarian, on my fully accepting them as humans, and on showing them that they can fully accept themselves and that I am very much interested in helping them do so. I am not interested in them personally, in the sense that I want to go to bed with them or be friends with them, but in helping them to overcome their problems.

With some clients, whom I realize are sad sacks – for example, older people who are probably not going to change very much – I go out of my way to show them that I think they are capable, competent and nice, and I sandwich in more complimentary remarks than I would do with younger and more capable clients. As a result, they are likely to think that I regard them as personally desirable, and they may like me very much because of this. I do this largely with the more limited people, not across the board, while with others who are less limited I'm more likely to stick to a more authoritative form of rapport building. Mostly, I think that my clients tend to view me as a nice, competent, helpful teacher much more than as a friend or lover.

W.D. Would I be correct in assuming that because the emphasis in RET is on helping clients to overcome their problems outside the therapy sessions and the main type of rapport relates to the role of the therapist as an authoritative teacher, that transference reactions on the part of the client are not as frequently found in RET as they might be in, for example, psychoanalytical therapy?

A.E. Yes, but in RET we recognize different kinds of transference. First, there is the classical transference, where clients presumably feel and act towards the therapist as they did towards their original parents. They see the therapist as a father or mother figure and overgeneralize from the past. Some people, though by no means all, do that, and it comes from a cognitive error called overgeneralization: 'The therapist looks like my father and is about the same age, therefore he must be just like my father, and I love him or hate him because he is like my father.' If we find out that this kind of inaccurate generalization is occurring, we try to show clients what they are doing and help them to give it up. We don't put them through a deliberate transference neurosis or anything like that, because that would tend to reinforce their disturbed tendencies to overgeneralize. It is quite foolish of them to love or hate their therapist because he has one or two traits similar to those of their parents; and one object of therapy is to help them change this kind of foolish thinking.

The second kind of transference, which it has come to mean today in non-Freudian therapy like that developed by Karen Horney and Harry Stack Sullivan, is that when clients have a relationship with the therapist right now, in the present, they re-enact with the therapist some of the thoughts, feelings and behaviours they do in their own life and in their outside relationships. As therapists, we then point out, 'Well, now that you are acting this way with me, don't you act similarly with your mate or other people? Isn't there a relationship between how you behave in therapy and in your outside life?' So we find out things in the therapy sessions that could be important in the outside world. If clients are anxious with me, I may use that as an example of how they are anxious in their other relationships. So by relating to me, clients may undergo a learning process and discover some important errors and learn how to correct them. This is sometimes called a corrective emotional experience.

On the other hand, when clients fall in love with their therapist – a female client with a male therapist or a male client with a female therapist – I find that this is *not* usually because of their past or because the therapist is like their parents. Rather, it occurs because right now, in the present, the therapist likes them, helps them, is attractive, is bright, and has other desirable traits. So it's a real love relationship, not a fantasy that mimics their past, and one that had better be acknowledged and taken care of so that it does not interfere with the therapy. With my clients, I try to discuss it and work it through, or I may recommend that the client see another therapist.

W.D. Has it ever happened that you and one of your female clients have become quite fond of one another?

A.E. That's happened in a number of cases. Most of my female clients are sad sacks and I may lust after them if they are attractive women, but I never think of having a relationship with them because they are quite disturbed and I realize that if I were personally involved with them they would soon act obnoxiously. I can see right away that if I met such a woman socially she would be nice for a brief affair but not for a steady relationship.

But every once in a while some client is absolutely terrific and is the kind of person that, if I met her socially and if I were not mated already, I would get very attracted to. Sometimes she seems to relate to me somewhat similarly and we have quite a good relationship in therapy. Incidentally that hasn't happened too much recently, because I'm much older than my attractive female clients right now. So I may get attracted to them but they are not going to get that attracted to me. In the past, when I was younger, this happened much more often, which just shows that transference tends to be based on reality rather than on female clients loving me because I resemble their fathers! When clients do fall in love with me we usually discuss this, agree that sex-love intimacy between clients and their therapist is unethical, and either work through their strong feelings for me or else I refer them to another therapist. Because RET teaches people that they do not *need* what they strongly *want*, it can show clients that no matter how intensely they love a therapist, they do not *have* to engage in a personal relationship with him or her. Incidentally I have done RET over the years with a number of my female partners with whom I was having a sex-love relationship. When they got upset, I would do therapy with them, and often help them considerably. When I was practising psychoanalysis, trying to analyse my sex-love partners didn't work very well. But doing RET with them was much easier and better! Because RET is so scientific and practical, it can even work with close friends and lovers!

W.D. My experience is that whenever I've tried to do that with my wife it isn't really what she wants, she wants a hug or some comfort. She doesn't want RET!

A.E. Yes, that's right; and I've sometimes got into trouble with women friends who say, 'Don't use that RET on me! I want you to listen and be sympathetic!' But then, at other times, when they really wanted help with their emotional problems, I was able to help them considerably with RET discussions that were almost exactly like those I usually have with clients.

I'll tell you a story about this very attractive female client, about 25, divorced with a young child, whom I was encouraging to go out with men and to work on her hang-ups. It was going well for several sessions but then she said, 'I can't talk to you freely any more because I'm very attracted to you, and here we are talking about my sex life with other men. I have great difficulty in doing that because I am really attracted to you, would much rather go to bed with you than with them, and am embarrassed about telling you some of the details of the sex I have with them.' Because I was attracted to her, too – she was very bright and charming – I said honestly, 'I am attracted to you, too. But this is therapy, so we can't do anything about having any personal relationship. If you really do have trouble in keeping talking to me, I will refer you to another therapist and that will be that. Give it some thought.' So she came back a week later and seemed to have no trouble talking to me about her sexual activities or anything else. I pointed this out, and asked, 'What have you decided to do about seeing me when you find it so hard to talk about your dates with other men?' She replied, 'Oh, I've changed my attitude completely. Because while talking to you during our last session, I discovered you were older than I thought you were [I was about 45 at the time]. You mentioned getting your Masters and PhD degree eight years after you got your college degree and I was going by your degrees on the wall in the waiting room and I thought you were eight years younger than you are. My ex-husband was too old for me – he didn't want to run around town as much as I did nor do other energetic things. So I said to myself, if Dr Ellis is older than my ex-husband and *he* was too old for me, obviously Dr Ellis would not make a good marital partner. So now I am no longer in love with you!'

Incidentally her case was really a classic case disproving the

Freudian idea of transference. Because her father was a physician and about my age, so that Freud would have absolutely insisted that she fell in love with me because I was similar to her nice father! But actually, as soon as she found out my real age, her love for me vanished, and we went on very nicely with the therapy. She may have still been attracted to me and I to her; but it didn't matter because she wasn't seeing me as a potential husband, which I think is what a lot of women do with their therapists. So that shows that her feelings for me were based on reality much more than on Freudian transference theories. Many clients *realistically* fall for their therapist because, if they met them socially instead of therapeutically, he or she would be quite the kind of person they would like to mate with.

W.D. On that particular theme, maybe it's because you have written about your own sex life that the myth has grown up around you that you have slept with and had affairs with some of your clients. Could you set the record straight on this and perhaps speculate on some of the origins of that story?

A.E. Well, first of all, at least a couple of my disgruntled female clients have falsely put around stories that I slept with them. Sometimes because I *didn't* sleep with them they got disgruntled and then said after therapy was over that they slept with me. So that was partly the origin. Also, the rumour has been around for years, and still is, either that I've had five wives or else that I've had eight wives. People still believe that. I've said in public that it's not true, but because I am a sexologist and have written about sex and my love life, people do make up things.

The other rumour, that I haven't heard recently but that was around for a long time, is that I've slept with most of my gay clients! That is really funny! I supposedly sleep with practically all my attractive female clients and I sleep with many gay clients! These things easily get invented and, when you are a sexologist, I think they much more often get invented. But actually I haven't had sex with any of my female clients; and certainly not with any of my male clients, because even if it were ethical to do so, which it definitely isn't, I have never been interested in having sex with men. I certainly would have liked to go to bed with a number of my female clients because they were bright and attractive women, but I merely acknowledge that desire in my own head and only get on with the therapy.

When my women clients bring up their desire to have sexual or other kinds of personal relationships with me, we discuss it and I have my standard answers (which I haven't had to go through for a few years now because of my age): 'No, no matter how much we may personally like each other, having an affair is impossible. It ruins the therapeutic relationship, almost always leads to harmful results, and is therefore highly unethical. Although we may both want it and may feel greatly deprived if we don't have it, there is no way in which we can have sex with each other.'

W.D. Do you regret that it doesn't come up any more?

A.E. It would be nice if they were as attracted to me sexually as they were in the old days. The same thing goes with the women I meet socially. In the old days a number of them, maybe because they wanted to be celebrity-fuckers, were attracted to me, and now practically none of them are, and that's too bad! I manage to survive very nicely in spite of that 'terrible' handicap!

W.D. Let's go on to the next principle.

A.E. The next principle is helping clients to reframe things when they are upset about them. When people are disturbed they only see the bad side of certain things and grossly exaggerate that side. If they get rejected they think it's *horrible*, that they will *always* be rejected, and that they are essentially *rejectable*. In RET, we show them that these are definitional, non-verifiable philosophies, and indicate how they can Dispute that kind of exaggerated thinking.

One technique is to show clients that when anything goes wrong, it usually has its good side. As I often point out to my clients and at my workshops, 'If you go out socially and you soon get rejected when you are looking for a mate, that's good! Because you then *quickly* get rid of a person who is not for you! Remember that if he or she seemed to accept you at the beginning and then later rejected you, that would be worse. So it's *good* to get rejected right away! The same thing occurs when you are selling something and you call up a customer and immediately get turned down. That's good! – because you get released right away to make other potential sales.' I also humorously point out: 'When you get rejected in love, you had better look at the good side: you could have married that person and had nine ugly and stupid children!'

In many respects it's good to fail, because you learn by failing and by trial and error. So we teach people in RET to look not only at the good side, but also at the good side of the bad side. Even the bad feelings that happen to you – the horror, the anxiety, the terror, the depression – have a good side because they give you the challenge of not feeling miserable and depressed, but only feeling appropriately sorry and disappointed about them. And *knowing* that you can almost invariably keep yourself from abject terror and depression, can lead to your actually feeling *happy*. Anybody can be happy when good things happen. But if you can really see that you are in control of your emotional destiny and are able to be undepressed when things are at their worst, that's reframing your emotional reactions. So in several ways RET helps people to look differently at the bad things of their life and thereby to make themselves unmiserable, and sometimes even happy, when they occur.

W.D. Is there any therapeutic value in helping clients to see the bad aspects of the good things in life?

A.E. The answer is yes. I usually wouldn't bother to do this because damned few of my clients would ask me to show them this. But when we work on self-esteem and my clients say, 'I won this tennis match and I felt good about myself', then I show them right away that that has a bad aspect. Because if you feel good about *yourself* for winning, how are you going to feel about your same *self* for losing? Pretty *awful*! So RET often helps people to give up some 'good' feelings, such as self-righteousness, that often lead to later self-downing and other poor results.

W.D. What is the next principle you want to deal with?

A.E. The next principle is teaching philosophy. Our assumption in RET is that if people had thoroughly sensible, rational philosophies, they would be much less disturbed. They would have a hard time being neurotic if they had a set of rational philosophies. One that we teach frequently is the philosophy of tolerance – you always accept other humans even though they do rotten things. You forgive other people, not necessarily what they *do*, but you forgive *them*. Then you are more likely to accept and forgive *yourself*, but not your *acts*, even when you behave abominably.

RET also favours the philosophy of long-range hedonism, which is the opposite of that of low frustration tolerance. You go for both the pleasure of the moment *and* the pleasure of the future, rather than sacrificing more important future gains for immediate gratification.

An important philosophy of RET is that all humans, including you the client, are fallible; and therefore there is no way in which you will never make mistakes, even big mistakes. So you had better accept yourself as very fallible because that accords with reality. That's what humans are – fallible fucked-up beings. Too bad – but that's it! Actually, they *are* not fuck-ups but they *act* in foolish ways much of the time.

There's the philosophy that Reinhold Niebuhr expounded – 'Give me the courage to change what I can change, the serenity to accept what I cannot change, and the wisdom to know the difference between the two.' AA has taken this over and RET also endorses it. Another philosophy is that there doesn't seem to be any magic in the world. It's mainly a question of work and practise. You don't have a fairy godmother, God, or any other supernatural force to help you be in touch with the secret soul of the universe or to tap into magical energy forces that will completely change and cure you. You had better give up that superstition and rely on your own creative abilities – your own thoughts, feelings and behaviours – to change yourself and unfortunate conditions.

Then there is the philosophy of responsibility. You aren't ever a rotter for doing anything wrong. But still, you acted foolishly or immorally and you are responsible for what you did. So don't cop out and say you didn't behave badly – against your and your social group's interests. If you did, you did. But then don't beat yourself for being responsible for bad acts, either. Your responsibility for your errors never equals your wormhood. You are also largely responsible for your feelings, so don't say somebody else *made* you feel a certain way. Fortunately, you did. So, happily, you can change the way you feel.

Finally, there's the philosophy I mention in my book on *Executive Leadership* (Ellis 1972c), the two great words which will rid you of most of your neurotic disturbance, if you really believe them: '*Tough shit!*' Frequently, that's the way it just unfortunately *is*. Tough! Whether you like it or not. And you had better try to be a happy human, in spite of many crummy events that you create or that others foist on you. So things are often difficult. Don't pretend that they're not. But – *tough shit*. What are you now going to do to correct them – or, if uncorrectable, live with them and *still* lead a reasonable happy existence?

W.D. I think critics of RET would say that most clients come into therapy wanting to overcome specific problems and here you are trying to teach them philosophies of life which they may not be interested in.

A.E. That's right, you're quite right, that may be a handicap of RET. But don't forget that because we are also practical, pragmatic and problem-solving, and even at times advice-giving, and because we invariably go back to people's undesirable activating events and try to help them change them, with our realistic *tough shit* philosophy we are actually giving people an extra option of learning to cope with circumstances when they are *not* changeable. If therapists just concentrate on changing clients' circumstances, they're being Pollyanna-ish, because they're implying that every problem has a good solution and that they can show the client what it is. That, alas is a false premise, because sometimes problems *don't* have a good solution. If RETers gave philosophical solutions *instead* of practical ones we would truly be open to legitimate criticism. Actually, we do both – help people to change *within* their family, business and social system and then help them to change the system itself. I therefore call RET a double systems therapy, as distinct from some of the other systems therapies.

W.D. Is there a danger that RET therapists might stray over the border and try to indoctrinate their clients with the philosophy of RET?

A.E. Oh yes, and we would be opposed to that. For example, in my chapter 'The philosophic implications and dangers of some popular behavior therapy techniques' (Ellis 1983), I show that you can reinforce people for having a better philosophy, but then do they really have it by themselves? I quote in that chapter the statement of Maimonides that if we reward people for reading they will do more reading, but they won't necessarily enjoy the reading or do it because *they* really like to read. So in RET we do not only try to help clients to change their philosophy for better immediate practical results, but also so that they can think it through for themselves, can *like* having their new attitudes, and can make the kind of profound philosophic change that will lead to a more enjoyable later existence. That is why we do not favour their unthinkingly parroting nice coping statements as other cognitive-behaviour therapists often have them do.

W.D. Very occasionally on your tapes and demonstrations I hear you saying to clients, 'Don't take my word for it, think it through for yourself.' But having listened to a lot of your tapes and a lot of your Friday Night Workshops, I think the criticism could be laid at your door that you don't encourage independent thinking in your clients *enough*. It seems that right from the start you are encouraging them to adopt the rational philosophy, and isn't that a danger if as you said earlier, one of the major aspects of the therapeutic relationship is your being authoritative rather than authoritarian? One of the dangers of working with somebody who is authoritative is that clients may not think things through for themselves and may just take them on your authority.

A.E. That always is a danger and I do several things to try to counteract it. First, from time to time, when clients say things like, 'I can put off my immediate gratification in order to get long-range gains' I stop and challenge them, 'Why is that so?' I force them to thinkingly substantiate their correct answers, not just to parrot them. Second, I emphasize their continuing to actively *Dispute* their irrational Beliefs and not merely take on *my* rational philosophies. Third, I encourage them to vigorously, often implosively, act against their self-defeating and to actualize their self-helping philosophies. If they say, for example, 'Yes, risk-taking is better than safely sitting on my ass. Nothing ventured nothing gained' – which is one of the philosophies of RET – I respond, 'OK, what are you going to *do* to actualize that view, to put it into practice? Because unless you practise it many times, you won't really believe it and feel it. You'll just be giving it lip-service.' Fourth, to my clients who believe 'I don't have to perform well even though I'd like to do so', I frequently say, 'Fine! Now what can you *do* to really believe that?'

W.D. Is that partly to encourage clients to conduct an experiment to see if acting on that philosophy really does bring better results?

A.E. Yes, and as a matter of fact you've just brought up another RET technique which is to encourage experimentation. I often say to clients, 'Now don't take what I say on faith. Go out and try it and see how it works for you. Unless you experiment, you won't be convinced that rational philosophies really work and you won't change that much.'

W.D. Now, a major part of teaching RET philosophy is the use of psycho-educational materials.

A.E. Yes, RET has been a pioneer in psycho-educational materials since its earliest beginnings. At first, I would give my clients some of my professional articles to read and they benefited so much from going over them that I began to favour bibliotherapy. While I was concocting RET, I wrote *The American Sexual Tragedy* (Ellis 1954), a manual on sex and love relations, and used that with my clients. My idea was that if people could benefit from the teaching I did in my therapy sessions, they could also benefit through the written word. So I gave them pamphlets and then in 1956 (a year after I started RET) I wrote *How to Live with a Neurotic* (Ellis

1957), my first book on RET, which has steadily been in print since it was first published. I also began to have clients refer themselves because they first read my books and articles. So I continued to publish a good many self-help books and I found that they helped people enormously when I (and a number of other therapists) recommended them to supplement therapy. So far the most effective is my latest self-help book, *How to Stubbornly Refuse to Make Yourself Miserable about Anything – Yes Anything!* (Ellis 1988). I deliberately wrote it very simply so that people can quickly and easily learn some of the main elements of RET. So psycho-educational techniques are an intrinsic part of rational-emotive therapy.

As I pointed out in a recent talk to the American Psychological Association's 1990 Convention, 'The Advantages and Disadvantages of Therapy Self-Help Materials', several recent studies are quite significant. One shows that when older depressed people used self-help materials on how to overcome depression – by Peter Lewinsohn, David Burns, myself, and others – they improved significantly more than a control group which didn't use this self-help material. Another study shows that when therapists were asked whether self-help books help their clients, about 70 per cent say that they frequently recommended them and found that they were helpful. So we are getting increasing evidence in favour of self-help material.

The Institute for Rational-Emotive Therapy in New York provides our clients with books, pamphlets, audio and video cassettes, and other self-help materials and sells many thousands of these every year. It also presents many workshops, lectures and other public presentations which teach people RET without their having to enter therapy, or in addition to therapy. Many people come to my famous weekly Friday Night Workshops and never have therapy sessions. Yet they often report considerable psychological improvement – as do others who listen to my RET tapes. So we find that RET self-help materials considerably help many clients and non-clients.

W.D. Let's go on to the next principle, which is changing clients' language.

A.E. Yes RET accepts the view of Alfred Korzybski who was one of the pioneers in language and who said that when we think crookedly, especially when we overgeneralize, our thought influences our language and then our language makes us think *more* crookedly. Irrational thinking and sloppy language continually interact. So when clients say, '*People* make me angry or upset', we interrupt them and say, 'No you'd better restate that: "*I* make myself angry or upset".' Or when they say, 'I *should* do well', we teach them to change their language to, 'I *had better* do well, but I don't *have* to do so'. If they say, 'I *can't* change', RET helps them say instead, 'It is *difficult*' for me to change, but not *impossible*'. So one of our techniques is to encourage clients to change their language and that helps many people.

W.D. What do you think would be the effect if you helped clients to change their language to a more rational language, but did nothing else?

A.E. Well, some clients are the kind of people who would internalize straighter language and also get themselves to *think* more rationally. But others would change their language by rote and therefore be helped relatively little.

W.D. The next principle you want to discuss is having clients teach RET to others. What is particularly therapeutic about that?

A.E. We have found out, as have many cults and religious groups, that when you teach things to others you tend to teach them better to yourself. Many teachers, following John Dewey, have discovered this, so it's not just a therapeutic principle. Consequently we often recommend that clients use RET with their friends and relatives. When I was a psychoanalyst, I told my clients, '*Don't* analyse your friends and relatives or you will help screw them up'. So they *did* analyse them and *did* help to screw them up. Now I say to clients, '*Do* use RET with people you know. Often it will help them to change, but even if they don't you will absorb it more yourself.' I have hundreds of cases now where people have told me, 'I helped my wife very much with RET', and where the wife came in and said, 'My husband helped me very much with RET'. But I have even more instances where, even when they didn't get it over that well to others, they absorbed it more themselves, as proselytizers often do. Back in the 1970s Jim Bard did a study of college students where two groups learned RET and one group used it with their friends while the other didn't. The students who used it with their friends improved significantly more on an irrational Beliefs test than those who didn't.

W.D. Are there dangers in this procedure?

A.E. Oh yes, there are always dangers. First of all, when you teach RET to others, you may not teach it correctly. You may put in an absolutistic form like, 'You must not use musts'. Or you may leave out many of the finer points. Also, when you teach it to others they may say, 'What do *you* know?' They think they require an authoritative therapist to teach it rather than their friends. Friends may edit you out, or you may even get into trouble with them: 'Don't used that goddamned RET on me! Keep it to yourself!' Several poor results may ensue, but experience has shown me that more good than bad things happen with RET proselytizing.

W.D. OK. The next principle I have got down here that you want to talk about is modelling.

A.E. As Albert Bandura has shown, people often learn by therapeutic modelling, especially in the case of children. RET hypothesizes that when the therapist does not get upset when the client behaves badly – for example, berates the therapist, comes late, or doesn't pay the bills – the therapist then models appropriate behaviour for the client to learn. This works in many respects. For example in my Friday Night Workshops I interview people in public and show volunteer clients how to use RET. Afterward, a good many people come up to me and say, 'Dr Ellis, I never volunteered here because I am still afraid to get up in public and talk about my personal problems. But I have seen that many of the problems other people brought up were similar to mine; and when you showed them what to do about their difficulties, how to think differently, I started doing the same thing in my own life. Now my problems have significantly improved!' These people obviously gained by modelling or vicarious therapy. So if the therapist models the application of RET philosophies in front of the client, he or she may effectively get across these philosophies. When an RET practitioner refuses to get upset and blame the clients for their destructive behaviour, these clients often see that they don't have to damn themselves.

W.D. What are the dangers of modelling?

A.E. Well, the client may pick up the wrong idea. For example I may show that I forgive the client as a person for something, and clients may mistakenly conclude, 'Dr Ellis thinks that what I did was right'. Actually I was trying to show them that *they* are OK even though what they *did* was wrong. Modelling is an imprecise form of communication, and I don't think Bandura or others point that out enough. Therefore, if you are going to model sensible behaviour, you had better also make sure through other teaching methods as well that clients pick up the right messages.

W.D. The next principle you want to talk about is encouraging clients to learn from sessions by recording and then listening to their sessions.

A.E. Yes, we allow clients to record their own sessions and many of them record practically every single session they have at our clinic at the Institute in New York. Though some clients then don't listen to their recordings, others listen to each session at least once. Some do it five or ten times. They listen while vacuuming or they listen in their car when caught in traffic. Frequently they report that they got more out of the recording than out of the original session, because during the session they were talking back and arguing and distracting themselves, while when listening to the recording they are just listening to themselves and to their therapist. They also hear, on the recording, how foolishly their negative philosophies are, and therefore are more inclined to change them.

W.D. With some clients, I have found that when they listen to their recordings they make themselves worse because they focus on how they sound and they say things like, 'How terrible I sound and what a jerk I am for saying these things!' So I suggest we discontinue the recording for a while because they just use it as another opportunity to disturb themselves.

A.E. Yes, that's a good point. But when they bring up how stupid they sound, I make it grist to the therapeutic mill. Because it gives me an opportunity to say, 'By all means listen to the recording and focus on how stupidly you *acted*. But you don't have to put *yourself* down for acting like that!' So it can even be turned to therapeutic advantage if they flagellate themselves for the way they sound on tape.

W.D. The next principle is the use of stories, fables and analogies.

A.E. Stories, fables and analogies are dramatic ways of getting a point over. RET is largely a teaching or persuasive form of therapy. We are trying to persuade people to change their attitude, to change their feelings, to change their behaviour, because even if they knew *what* to do before they came to therapy they weren't *doing* it. So we push them and persuade them, and one way to persuade people is to use stories, fables, analogies, poems, jokes and other literary devices to get a point across. Many plays, George Bernard Shaw's plays for example, are propaganda plays.

A story I frequently use is the one about the two Zen Buddhist monks who come to a stream. One is an old man of 90 and the other is a young monk of 20 and they are both sworn to abstinence. There is a beautiful, luscious young woman standing by the stream and she says to them, 'Masters, the stream is flooded and I can't swim. Will you help me across?' The young monk is horrified, because he will have to pick her up and carry her in his arms across the stream, and says, 'No, madam, I can't do that – it's against my vows to touch a woman.' But the old man thinks for a moment and then picks her up in his arms and carries her across the stream. She thanks him and the two Zen Buddhists go on with their journey. The young man can't stand what the old monk has done and says to him, 'Master, how could you do a terrible thing like that – picking up that beautiful young woman, letting her put her lovely arms around your neck and her luscious breasts close to your breast – and *carry* her across the stream?' The old man replies, 'My son, *you're* still carrying her!' This story beautifully dramatizes how the old monk committed a sin – and dropped it; while the young man, who had done no wrong except in his head, was determined to hold on to it forever! I often use it to forcefully show people how they hang on to their sabotaging self-statements when they can choose to give them up.

W.D. That particular method seems to be quite in vogue these days. Milton Erickson used to tell his clients fables and stories and claimed he was somehow talking to their unconscious. Is there a danger that the client may not see the point in the analogy?

A.E. I can almost see just by looking at them whether they get it, or I may ask them, 'Do you get this?' If not, I explain it to them. Now, with Milton Erickson, first of all I don't think he by any means was talking to clients' deep unconscious and thereby helping them therapeutically. He was mainly dramatizing and persuading people to do what they otherwise would be reluctant to do. He was such a great raconteur, in fact, that I suspect that he fictionalized some of his therapy results. I agree that in the cases he reports he sometimes cleverly got his point over. But I would guess that in many of his failed – and largely unreported – cases, his clients' 'unconscious' really picked up a wrong, harmful message. I often use dramatic and forceful stories with my clients, but they are aimed at their *conscious* mind, not their unconscious! And I use them to help these clients make very *conscious*, lasting changes in their basic irrational philosophies.

W.D. And would you advise that this technique be used sparingly or liberally?

A.E. I think that a few good stories, which the therapist knows from experience go over well can be used frequently. But don't overdo it!

W.D. Now the next principle is the use of cognitive distraction.

A.E. Yes, it has been found over the years that when people are anxious about anything, they tend to dwell on it, exacerbate their anxiety and make things much worse. Now the elegant RET solution is to show clients how to ask, 'What am I telling myself to make myself anxious?' and to have them Dispute their panic-creating Beliefs until they give them up. But sometimes it's useful to get clients to allay their anxiety temporarily by almost any kind of effective distraction – such as their using Edmund Jacobson's progressive relaxation technique, Yoga, meditation, breathing exercises, entertainment, looking at TV, reading, et cetera. There are scores of possible distractions, and if they really concentrate on one or more of these they will temporarily feel better. RET uses distraction, especially with people who are panicked, because they are often incapable of Disputing well and of believing rational self-statements. We encourage them to use various kinds of distraction techniques to calm down and be unpanicked, and then to use Disputing and other RET methods. But we rarely use distraction technique by themselves, without other aspects of RET. One of the best distraction methods, that I often recommend, especially for very anxious and obsessive-compulsive clients, is that they get a long-term vital absorbing interest, that will distract them generally from their panic states. But I also recommend that they become absorbed in doing RET with themselves, which may be both distracting and curative.

In regard to distraction I often tell the story of a woman who gave me a lift back to New York city from a New York state workshop that I had given. She was a charming young woman of around 29 or so, very bright and attractive, and a Yoga teacher. She taught Yoga for a living, and did it herself twice a day for twenty minutes and got very relaxed and felt good after it. And yet this charming young woman of 29 was horribly afraid that she was an unlovable old maid who would never marry! All the Yoga, all the distraction she had used for several years, hadn't affected her philosophy of self-downing or helped her to change it. So distraction techniques often work, but they are usually palliative and rarely lead to the kind of profound philosophical change that RET tries to promote.

W.D. Now would skill training also be classed as a technique like distraction in this respect? You have said that it's better to do skill training after Disputing irrational Beliefs.

A.E. I usually start with philosophic Disputing and then may add skill training, especially because many people don't need training in special skills once they use RET to make themselves less disturbable. They already know how to study, how to have sex, and how to communicate. But some people who nicely Dispute their irrational Beliefs, and are no longer afraid to socialize or go for a job interview, may actually *not* know how to communicate well. So I may give them social relations training, interpersonal skills training, communications training, and so on. At the same time, there are some skills that people had better learn right away – such as writing résumés and job interviewing if they are unemployed – so I may start on the skill training during the very first session.

W.D. What specific disadvantages do you think skill training has in rational-emotive therapy?

A.E. The main disadvantage is that when a therapist overemphasizes it, clients may never get around to the main business of changing their irrational philosophies. They may become so entranced with learning communication skills that they often fail to Dispute their irrational Beliefs, such as 'I *must* not communicate poorly and if I do, I'm an inadequate person!' They function better but still have self-damning and awfulizing philosophies when they don't. Thus, I see many people with sex problems and if I show them some effective techniques, they often leave after a few sessions because they are doing much better sexually. But actually they may by no means have ameliorated their basic anxiety or their other cognitive-emotional problems.

W.D. The next principle concerns the use of reinforcement and penalties. Could you say a little bit about why that is an important practical principle in RET?

A.E. RET particularly emphasizes homework – cognitive, emotive and behavioural homework – and of course many people only do it partly, or don't do it all, or do it once in a while. For instance, once in a while they'll go out to socialize, but only infrequently. Therefore, we often find it useful to do contingency management or operant conditioning. So only *after* they do their homework – such as date others, go for a job interview, register for school, or write a report or paper – do they *then* engage in a self-selected enjoyable pursuit. But as I frequently say at my workshops, studies of successful operant conditioning or reinforcement are largely based on experiments with children; and children are crazy – they'll do anything for M&Ms [Smarties]! With adults, sometimes reinforcement works beautifully and that's fine. But when it doesn't work, especially with the DCs (difficult customers), RET tries to get them to agree to workable penalties, such as burning money or sending it to a cause that clients hate.

None the less, even with reinforcements and penalties people rebel against doing therapeutic homework; and they also set reinforcers and penalties, agree to enact them, and then refuse to do so. Therefore, RET practitioners go back to Disputing clients' irrational Beliefs about their homework. Thus, when they fail to carry out agreed-upon assignments, we ask, 'What are you telling yourself *not* to do your homework?' Usually we find them irrationally saying, 'It's hard, it's *too* hard! It *shouldn't* be this hard! How *awful* that I have to do such unpleasant things to get better.' So, using RET, we show them how to (1) change their anti-homework Beliefs; (2) use penalties and reinforcements; (3) if these are not adhered to, we persuade clients to get a friend or relative to monitor their reinforcing and penalizing themselves. If we persist at encouraging clients to do cognitive, emotive and behavioural homework, we ultimately enable most of them to do it some of the time, and some to do it without any sweat and with no use of reinforcements and penalties.

W.D. Presumably you have some difficult customers who won't use the reinforcement *or* the penalties, *and* won't get other people to help them, but just will continue in their own way?

A.E. That's right, they won't do it on their own, nor arrange for somebody to monitor them. If they steadily refuse to do any homework, I just tell them unangrily, 'Well, if you are not going to do any, you're not going to change. If you want to get over your fear of elevators there is no way you are going to get over over it by *not* going in an elevator, so if you stubbornly refuse to do so, you will prolong your phobia forever. You are entitled, of course, to do that. But you're just unethically sabotaging yourself.' 'Unethically?' they ask. 'Yes, you're foolishly choosing to do *yourself* in. What could be more unethical than that?' If they still won't do anything like homework, they usually eventually quit therapy after making only limited gains. Too bad! – but you (and I!) can't win them all.

3 GENERAL ISSUES

WINDY DRYDEN At this point, Al, I want to cover a wide range of general issues and get your views on them. Some of these issues were suggested to me by other people. Now to start with it would be interesting to hear what your views are about the therapeutic value of diagnostic category systems like DSM-III-R and to what extent you use these in your own work and encourage other therapists to use them.

ALBERT ELLIS Well, I use the DSM-III-R largely for insurance purposes, because we have to put it on the insurance forms. I think it's a reasonably accurate description and I don't have anything much against it because it sticks to rather overt behaviours and states if a person has most of these overt behaviours he or she is severely depressed, panicked, borderline or has some other specific diagnosis. Sometimes, it has relatively little use in therapy, because highly depressed and anxious individuals may have similar irrational Beliefs, and revealing and Disputing these Beliefs may be more important than giving them a diagnostic label. But knowing how severely disturbed a person is can be very useful, particularly in the case of psychotic and borderline clients, who may be referred for medication, together with somewhat prolonged RET. I personally, during my first sessions, diagnose my clients as neurotic, borderline, borderline-plus (not too far from psychosis), psychotic and organic. The reason I do so is mainly to show myself how difficult it will probably be to help these clients change. I can help most of the neurotics change with relative ease. But with the borderlines, I can tell almost from the start that I am going to have trouble helping them to think rationally; with the borderline-plus clients, much more trouble; and with the psychotics I expect to have definitely limited gains. I may help the psychotics deal with their neurosis about their psychosis, show them how to accept themselves with their serious deficiencies. But, except with medication, I am not too likely to get them to eliminate their delusions, hallucinations, paranoid thinking, and other largely biologically based psychotic manifestations. So I make my own diagnosis, but it is largely in terms of how severely disturbed my clients are and how much medication they will probably require. The more disturbed they are, the more I make a mental note that I had better work harder.

In addition, I think in terms of specific traits that may hinder therapy. For example, certain people don't listen too well during their therapy session, so I will ask them to record each session and listen to it several times afterwards. Other clients don't do their self-monitoring and their homework, so I will emphasize the homework more with them, and may get them to use friends and relatives for extra outside monitoring. Depending on what my clients' diagnosis and handicaps are, and what individual characteristics they have, I will treat them quite individually.

W.D. What is your view of using clients' response to therapy as a way of assessing their degree of disturbance?

A.E. I think that one of the very best forms of assessment is how clients respond from the first session onwards to therapy. Neurotics very frequently start responding pretty well after a few sessions. After about five or six sessions you can start convincing them that they really do upset themselves and are capable of not doing so, and they start doing some good homework. The borderlines often do not clearly acknowledge or use the *ABC*s of RET; the borderline-plus clients have even more difficulty, as they are often quite confused and disorganized; and the psychotics often don't react well to active-directive Disputing until they have had many RET sessions. So I often diagnose people not by their presenting symptoms but by how they react to therapy. Many years ago, Paul Hoch diagnosed borderline personalities as pseudoneurotics. I think he was right, and I think that perhaps the best way of diagnosing them is by using an active-directive form of therapy like RET, to see what kinds of resistance often underlie their pseudoneurotic reactions.

W.D. To what extent do you think there may be a danger of concluding that a person is more disturbed than they really are because of how they react to RET? Alternatively, they may just not relate to RET as well as they may to other psychotherapeutic approaches.

A.E. But I take that into account. Because if a client works very hard – for example to get in touch with their feelings instead of getting in touch with their ideas and philosophies about their feelings – I often note to myself: 'This is a hard worker, who may not be too disturbed, and there is a good chance we will be able to collaborate in helping him or her.' While if a client refuses to work at RET, and perhaps has had years of psychoanalysis, Reichian, or Gestalt therapy, and never worked at that either, then I would initially diagnose him or her as being more seriously disturbed. But it doesn't matter much if I wrongly diagnose clients as more disturbed than they actually are, because then I will merely work harder to help them – which is one of the main reasons I diagnose them in the first place – to guess how hard I shall have to work with them. And no matter how difficult I find them to be, I practically never give up; I just try to work harder and try to persuade them to work harder. Then we can see how justifiable my diagnosis is.

W.D. Apart from instances where the person may be psychotic and refuses to take medication, are there any other circumstances whereby after assessing a client you would refuse to take them on for therapy?

A.E. Yes, there are some non-psychotics who refuse to take medication, and whom I occasionally refuse to see. For example, severely depressed suicidals are not psychotic, but sometimes I won't see them unless they see a psychiatrist too, and get medication. I think it is unethical and too risky not to push them to get multiple help. Bipolar manic-depressives, again, are not psychotic but can go off the wall without lithium or other medication, so I often push them to see a psychopharmacologist as we work with RET. When they are really manic, I usually won't see them unless they also take medication.

W.D. What boundaries do you draw in terms of whether or not you would see friends, family members or colleagues as clients in therapy?

A.E. My rule is that I just about never see my friends or colleagues regularly for therapy but I may see them for a session or two. Just recently an acquaintance of mine, a psychologist whom I have known for years, came to New York with his very close friend, another psychologist, to talk to me for a couple of hours about their problems. They both have individual problems, and I talked to them and showed them how irrational they were being and what they could do to stop upsetting themselves. They were quite appreciative, but I didn't charge them. No, I don't see friends or acquaintances regularly. I see them once or twice and then if they want more therapy they get a regular therapist, preferably an RET therapist. I occasionally see our therapists who work at the Institute. They have regular group therapy, with which I am not involved, and they can deal at length with any problems there. But if they want one session gratis to talk about their personal problems, they come to see me this single time. Also, once therapy is over with my regular clients, the only ones I have as friends are those who later become therapists. But I don't have even mildly friendly contacts with my regular clients after therapy has finished. I think that therapists who become very friendly with ex-clients are verging on, or actually engaging in, unethical behaviour.

W.D. What reasons do you have for not taking on friends, family members and colleagues for ongoing therapy?

A.E. Well, it gets too complicated and can easily lead to unethical, legal and other difficulties. Clients, for example, offer me business deals, but because of possible conflicts of interest, I always refuse. Sometimes I have clients who marry and who graciously invite me to their wedding, especially when I have helped them to overcome their fears of relating. But I say, 'No, I always refuse to go to my clients' affairs because if I went to yours, and even if I never spoke to you there, I would meet your friends and relatives and might get involved with them. Then you might be afraid of my giving away confidential information about you or of my becoming so close to them that you couldn't be open in our sessions about your feelings for, and doings with, them.' So I have always been very careful about any social contacts with my clients or with their close associates.

W.D. Have you arrived at this because you have been burned in the past or has that always been your principle?

A.E. I don't remember being burned in the past. The one exception to this rule is that when in the past I've been going with a woman, having a relationship with her, I frequently unofficially give her RET, but she isn't an actual client, she isn't having regular sessions. I don't charge her or anything like that! I don't recall an instance where I got burned, but there could have been one. However, there have been a few instances where I saw husbands and wives, or brothers and sisters at the same time and where one of them upset themselves because they thought I favoured the other or was on the other's side. That's why I have another rule: that when I am seeing *X*, and *Y* wants to come to me, and *Y* is closely related to or associated with *X*, I never see *Y* without *X*'s consent. I give *X* priority, and sometimes *X* says, 'On no, I don't want you to see Y'. I then won't do so. Now if *X* consents, I tell him or her the advantages and disadvantages of my seeing both of them. One advantage is that I can learn more about each of them when I keep talking to both. A disadvantage is lack of confidentiality. So I say to both, 'It's OK with me if it's all right with both of you. But if at any time either of you becomes uncomfortable because I am seeing the other, then the one who was here first has the priority.'

W.D. In a similar way, presumably you don't for practical as well as therapeutic reasons believe in socializing with your clients?

A.E. Right, I have always been opposed to that kind of thing even before the American Psychological Association banned it in its code of ethics. This is because I observed some harmful effects when other therapists socialized with their clients. For example, many years ago I was asked by a psychological association to testify against a psychologist because every few months he invited all his clients to a big party and told them to bring their friends, not just to come alone, and at this party he would try to sell their friends on therapy. Somebody complained about him, and I was asked whether I knew about his practices and it just so happened that I did, because he had told me about them himself! He had also, to my surprise, once asked me, 'Do you get a lot of cards from your clients on Valentine's Day?' I answered, 'I don't recall ever getting any!' 'Oh, I get a lot of them,' he said, and I thought that was odd. I may get a few cards from my clients on my birthday, which they may discover by reading *Who's Who*, and around New Year's Day some of them send me nice cards. But it's not because we have a social relationship.

I also found out about the dangers of social intimacy through talking with other therapists. And, through my own therapy with clients, I discovered that they sometimes reported that their previous therapists had been very social, including having sex with them, and that this led to harmful results. So I found out about the wrongness of socializing with clients in these ways, rather than through my doing it myself and getting into trouble.

W.D. To what extent have you found the therapeutic process helpful to you as a person?

A.E. Well, I found out many years ago, when I was a psychoanalyst, that it wasn't very helpful. Because when I analysed the dreams, the free associations, and the past history of my clients I remembered things about myself and perhaps understood my personality a little better, but it really didn't help me very much with my personal problems. But as soon as I started using RET and began to talk my clients out of their self-defeating, irrational Beliefs, I frequently said to myself, 'Now look, you had better face it; you've got that same nutty idea too!' or 'You're acting in the same crazy self-defeating way as this client is. Now what are *you* going to do about changing?' So I found that the practice of RET helped me considerably, especially when I was younger and could more often use such help. Now that I have used RET on myself for three and a half decades, I don't think I require it that much any more.

I also discovered, from many RET therapists, that they got into RET because they learned about and started helping themselves with it; and the more they used RET with their clients the saner they became. Now maybe that applies to most therapists – as they talk to their clients, they also benefit themselves, but I think it's mainly because they are wittingly or unwittingly using some elements of RET and not merely because they are talking to clients. That would be my (somewhat prejudiced) hypothesis.

W.D. In general, what clients do you find most difficult to work with in therapy?

A.E. Well, let's see, one group are those who really didn't benefit from previous therapy and who, according to their stories, suffered from it. The way they often see it is, 'I'm only coming to therapy because I have to, but I have no faith in it. I've tried it before and it didn't work then. Once you've seen one therapist, you've seen them all. I'm sure you will do much the same thing as those other therapists did, so it's a waste of time.'

Another kind of difficult client is one who is philosophically and ideologically antagonistic to therapy – who believes that 'The only way I can improve is to help myself. Therapy can't do it for me. So yours may be a better form of therapy, but really people have to sort out things for themselves. I'm only here because I'm very severely depressed and because my mate (or doctor or friend) insisted that I come.'

Other resistant clients include those who are sent to therapy against their will. The parole board, or the probation department or the judge sends them, and they are only coming in order to avoid going to jail or suffer other penalties. Also, there are adolescents who don't think anything is wrong with them but are forced to see a therapist because their parents insist that they come.

Then there are the severely disturbed clients, especially the borderline-plus clients, who often are more or less unable to think straight. These people are allergic to straight thinking, and some are so constantly overwhelmed with severe panic and/or depression that they just won't stop and work at RET or other forms of therapy. And of course, there are the older people in their seventies and eighties who are set in their ways and are only coming to therapy because they are extremely disturbed but have no real intention to work at changing.

W.D. Well, let's have a look at each of those groups in turn, and perhaps you could describe what effective strategies you have found with them. Let's start off with the group who haven't benefited much from previous therapy. What have you tried to do with them?

A.E. I try to show them that their bad results came about because the therapy they had was itself ineffective, or their therapists weren't actually using an effective kind of therapy, or they really weren't working hard enough to change themselves. Sometimes they tell me about therapists who did peculiar things, had sex with them or bawled them out and told them they really were no good. So I say, 'Either your therapy or your therapist probably was ineffective. So why not give RET a chance, for a while – *experiment* with it, and I think (though I won't guarantee), that you'll find it's quite different from what you had before. Try it and see!' I encourage them to experiment, to give RET and me as their therapist a trial. Sometimes, for therapeutic reasons, I explain why their previous therapy didn't work and why RET probably will really help.

W.D. It sounds as if you try and get some distance between RET and the other therapy.

A.E. Yes, if I think it was really harmful, I may show why it was. I may say, for example, 'During your three years of psychoanalysis, you found many interesting things about your early childhood. But even if they were accurate, which they may not have been, did that insight really help you? Did it show you what you told yourself to *make yourself* disturbed about your unloving mother and your nasty brother? Or did it wrongly lead you to believe that *they*, at point *A* upset you, instead of the important point that you upset yourself *about* their poor behaviour?' In this way I sometimes *redo* their previous therapy in RET terms to show them how it *could* have been helpful but it actually *wasn't*.

W.D. Now let's have a look at the next group you mentioned, which is what I call the compulsively self-reliant.

A.E. Yes, they have the philosophy that it is practically shameful to seek therapy. So I say to them, 'It's too bad you can't find your way out of your emotional difficulties without outside help. It would be nice if you could do it yourself. But, look, so far you haven't. Millions of people like you never do and are much improved with therapy, sometimes supplemented with medication. It's not at all shameful to be seriously disturbed – only as we say in RET a real pain in the ass! If it were *shameful* to resort to therapy anyone doing so would be a rotten or inadequate *person* – and RET, of course, denies this self-downing concept. You may have a bad emotional *problem* but that never makes you a bad *individual*.' So I try to convince my compulsively self-reliant objectors to therapy, 'However anxious and depressed you are, you had better accept that unfortunate reality. Never say you *shouldn't* be disturbed, and never put *you* down for your *neurosis*. Instead of making you *less* self-reliant, RET actually helps you right now and we hope for the rest of your life, be *more* reliant on yourself to undo the circumstances that you have largely, and unwittingly, created.' In particular, RET emphasizes *self*-therapy more than almost all other therapy systems.

W.D. The third group you mentioned are clients who are sent to therapy or in other ways are reluctant – they are not coming under their own steam. How do you try to help them?

A.E. I actually have a lot of luck with them, especially the teenage 'thugs' who committed some offence, such as stealing or playing hookey from school and are therefore hauled in to see me to discover their motives and help them to keep out of further trouble. I ask them, 'What bothers you?' And they often say, 'Nothing'. 'Well,' I say, 'I understand that you haven't been to school for several weeks. How do you feel about that?' They reply, 'Fuck it. Who cares?' They don't think that was so bad; and they think that they shouldn't be forced to go to school – or to see me – when they don't want to do so.

Nothing daunted, I usually induce them to talk about some feeling they will acknowledge, such as hostility. They are mad at their parents, at the person who sent them to therapy, at their school, or at something else, and they think they are justified. But I try to show them how their anger screws them up and gets them poor results. But first I tend to agree with them about some of their pet peeves – agree that, quite probably their parents are a pain in the butt, that the school system is pretty crummy, and that it would be better if they were not unduly restricted. I won't disagree with them about their gripes, and often even agree that they are being treated unfairly.

But I show them that they are unnecessarily *upset* about this unfairness and are thereby foolishly rebelling and bringing about *more* injustice. I show them how not to be unduly upset and how to help themselves thereby to get less frustration and more of what they really want. I show them that I'm not here to damn them like their parents and teachers usually do, but fully to accept them as they *are* – and then to help them change their behaviour for their *own*, and not mainly for their parents' or teachers' sake. Especially with teenage 'thugs', I say a few 'shits' and 'fucks', and they are on my side! They see I am not identified with authority, but can appreciate *their* points of view.

I can speak to psychopaths and show them that I do not damn *them*, but only look askance at some of the things they *do*. I often convince them that they are screwing *themselves* up and had better stop being enraged and immoral for their *own* long-range happiness and not *merely* because society wants them to be less enraged and more moral. I get many of them to bring out some problem *they* would like to work on and that would help them, even when they won't acknowledge their wrongdoings and their insecurities. I show them I am not going to report back to the judge that they are no good and they should be put in jail forever. But I also show them how self-defeating their acts are and how they can get more pleasure and less pain in life with less hostile and psychopathic behaviour.

Because most antisocial clients are unconventional people and they see that I am not conventional either, that I am not a typical goody-goody therapist, and that I give them unconditional positive regard even when they are fucked-up, they can tell by my direct attitude that I am really here to help *them*, not just their parents or their school or society. I am really on their side, and somehow I convince most of them of that and therefore they are willing to work on some of the problems that *they* perceive that they have.

W.D. Now we come to the clients who are, in your terms, 'borderline-plus'.

A.E. The borderline-pluses are very disorganized, don't think very straight, and can easily go disturbedly round and round in their thoughts and feelings. Because they have so much trouble changing and have often not benefited from previous therapy, they easily conclude, 'I can't change! I'm hopeless!' I am able to work with them because I soon say to myself, 'Well, this is going to take a long time and I am not going to get ideal results. This client may well be borderline for the rest of his or her life. Now, let's see how I can at least help him or her to improve.' I have lesser goals with borderline personalities than I do with nice neurotics. If necessary, I use whatever will work, even notions that are not really that rational at times, because these clients sometimes may not listen to rational persuasion. I may therefore help them be irrationally Pollyanna-ish or to like themselves because (with my help) they do well at work, or at relating or at something else. I am somewhat different with them than I am with nice neurotics. But I do find that the majority of borderlines really hate themselves for their deficiencies – especially for their disturbances – so I work very hard to convince them that they can fully accept themselves *no matter what*! If I succeed at that, they become significantly less disturbed and happier – even though they still really have a borderline personality.

W.D. Finally you mentioned working with older people.

A.E. Yes, again I often have limited goals with these clients. Thus I see widows in their sixties and seventies who I can soon see are not going to change too much. So I have more limited goals with them than I would have if they were younger. I don't look for a profound psychological change or anything close to it, though I occasionally help bring this about. I just strive to help them overcome their current anxiety and depression and do so by often persuading them to use very forceful coping statements, such as: 'I know that I *can* conquer my anxiety!' and 'My children *do* have the right to neglect me, and it is frustrating but not *awful* if they do.' 'I think that I *will* meet a suitable life partner, but I can *still* lead a happy life if I never do!' I use some positive thinking techniques that I would use very sparingly with younger people because older clients may benefit from them more than they would with realistic self-statements.

With some older people, however, I am able to achieve a remarkable change quite quickly. I will give you an example. My client was a bright woman, in her late sixties, a widow, and had obviously paranoid ideas. 'You know,' she said during our first session, 'there must be something a little wrong with my thinking, but I really believe it's true that several people are after me, are tapping my phone, and are saying nasty things to each other about me. How can I handle this?'

I said to myself straight away, 'She is not going to agree that these are paranoid ideas, even though she vaguely knows that they may be. If I tell her she's paranoid, she'll just run away from therapy.' If she were younger I might say right off, 'Now, look, you are paranoid and you had better give up demanding that other people be nice to you and thus give up your paranoid thinking when they are not super-nice.' But she is not going to agree to that and may well conclude that *I'm* crazy. She's a bright woman, not a basket case, and she even knows there's something wrong, but she wants me to tell her how to handle it. She asks, 'What should I do when they start checking on my bank account and when they keep phoning me and then hanging up?' So I say, 'Well, the next time they phone and then hang up on you, or when they check on your bank account, just tell yourself very, very strongly, "Look, these people are crazy! They have a real problem! They are only persecuting me because they are really very nutty and I can't change that! So, screw it! Let them waste their time trying to bother me! I refuse to upset myself about these screwballs!"' She perks up and says, 'You know, that's a good way to handle it. Thank you very much!' I only have one session with her and at that session I reassure her very strongly that she can handle and not upset herself about the people who are supposedly persecuting her. I don't even try to change any of her paranoid ideas, but instead show her that even if they are correct (which I, of course, silently think they aren't) she can handle her persecutors. I haven't seen her again for therapy, but she comes fairly often to my Friday Night Workshops and she says she's getting along fine! Now I wouldn't do this kind of palliative, non-disputing RET with a younger or less rigid person. Rather, I would try for a much more elegant kind of solution. But with an older, devoutly paranoid client, I do the best I can with some highly inelegant methods.

W.D. Moving on now, have you had much experience in dealing with clients who experience sexual abuse in their childhood?

A.E. Oh yes, I have had a good number of incest cases over the years, usually involving the client's father or often their uncle.

W.D. What in your experience have been their major problems about this, and how have you tried to help them to get over these problems?

A.E. Ironically by no means all of them have a serious emotional problem about incest, as the literature partly misleadingly states. You see, I saw two sisters, one of whom had steady sex with her father between the ages of 8 and 11, was not at all upset by having it and only became depressed when the father was jailed for incest and taken away from her. The other sister, three years younger, never had sex with her father, but began to hate herself when she discovered the incest between her father and her sister because she felt that he had favoured the more attractive sister. Both these women, when I saw them as adults, easily achieved orgasm and had no sex problems with their husbands. But both were self-denigrators because their father and all the other men in their lives never loved them as totally and perfectly as these women strongly thought that they *absolutely should*. There were both arrant love slobs – as also was their brother, who had no incestuous dealings with their father, who hated himself after his school chums laughed at him for his lack of athletic prowess. At the same time, I've seen hundreds of people who had no incestual experiences, nor did their brothers or sisters, and who grew up to be exceptionally disturbed and had severe sex problems.

On the other hand, I've seen a large number of other clients who had incestuous relationships with their parents or with other close relatives and who had serious sex problems as well as emotional problems. Usually, I treat them by showing them that it was not the incest itself that made them emotionally disturbed – because not all individuals who were incestuously abused turn out to be neurotic or to be inadequate sexually. Rather it is the musts and shoulds they tell themselves about their being abused.

W.D. Such as?

A.E. Such as, 'My father *shouldn't* have forced me to have sex with him! What a thorough bastard he was! All men are just like him, so I won't let any of them have good sex with me now!' Or, 'I *should not* have let my uncle have sex with me! There must be something really wrong with me for allowing this. Maybe I even liked it at times, too. Shit – what a rotten person I really am!' Or 'If this were a fair world, as it *should* be, the sexual abuse of my childhood would never have occurred; what a horrible world it is! I *can't stand* living in it!'

W.D. One of the criticisms I have heard is that one of the dangers of using RET with people who have problems related to childhood abuse is that if you try to make them see they are disturbed because of the view they are taking about it, you can come across to them as being insensitive. To what extent would you agree with that?

A.E. That rarely happens. Theoretically you would think that would happen a lot, but it doesn't. Don't forget, I agree with sexually or physically abused individuals that they really were unethically dealt with. Thus, I may say, 'Your father (or your brother or your uncle) really did seriously abuse and wrong you. So let's not at all exonerate him. He abused you sexually and acted in an immoral, distinctly wrong way. He took advantage of you, badly exploited you, and indeed acted criminally. So we are not going to argue about that. But,' I tell them, 'there are many other people like you who were treated just as badly, or even worse, some of them were even beaten up savagely and maimed. Are they *all* seriously disturbed now, as a result of that treatment? Many, of course, are. But hardly *all*. So what happened to you and them was bad – *very* bad. But it is still possible, using RET, to stop horrifying yourself about it – to stop hating yourself and your father for this most unfortunate set of events.'

So I try to show sexually and physically abused clients that I empathize and sympathize with them about what happened but that they need no longer disturb themselves so much about it. If they are still terrified or horrified, they are keeping the early abuse alive by saying, 'Because my father abused me all men are no good!' or 'Sex is no good!' or 'I'm a dirty person!' or 'I'm undeserving of sex pleasure!' They may not agree that they can now stop upsetting themselves about past abuse and exploitation. But very few of them accuse me of being insensitive.

W.D. Now one of the aspects of the *ABC*s of RET is that when *C*, the Consequence, is a disturbed emotion, then that is an indication that a person has irrational Beliefs. What about clients who say that they just don't feel anything much, they're just numb or bland, and who talk about being out of touch with their emotions?

A.E. They often pick that out-of-touch-with-my-feelings idea from therapists and writers who keep telling them that because they are not sufficiently enraged about what happened to them, they are seriously deficient. For it is a common therapeutic fetish today that unless you are extremely enraged or depressed about bad things that happen to you you have only numbness and are out of touch with your *real* feelings. Some people, of course, naturally have few excited negative or positive feelings. Some schizoid or schizophrenic individuals, as Paul Meehl noted about thirty years ago, are naturally anhedonic and perhaps some healthier people are, too. Instead of living, as Thoreau noted, lives of quiet desperation, they just live quietly period. And I am not sure that there is anything radically wrong with their dull lives – unless they think, 'I *should*, I *must* have much more feeling than I actually have!' *Then* they make themselves disturbed! Anyway, some people are probably naturally little hedonic or anhedonic, just as other people easily become very involved with people and things and then *easily* feel very sad and regretful when things go wrong and quite excited and joyous when their lives go well.

W.D. So the implication is that anhedonic people don't necessarily have irrational Beliefs blocking them.

A.E. No, some of them just don't have strong feelings, but mainly mild ones. They are passive people – that's their way; and I try to show them it's OK to go through life that way as long as they are not depressed and horrified about their passivity and tell them, 'If you don't have as much feeling as other people, it might be nice if you got yourself intensively involved with something and developed more feeling. So by all means seek some more intense pleasures. But there is no reason why you *have* to do this. You can have a good life without overwhelming feelings.'

I had a man come in to see me the other day who lives what would be called a low-level life. He goes to work, comes home and mainly looks at TV. He doesn't want to push himself to do much more. He knows that he probably can push himself to live more excitably, but he can easily live without this kind of effort. He was feeling guilty about not being more involved and active, and I said to him, 'Look, if you really want to do so you can get yourself to lead a more enjoyable life. But if you don't mind just looking at television and doing a little light reading well, that's OK, you really don't *have* to live a vibrant life to make you think you are an acceptable person.'

Other people who are presumably not in touch with their feelings are those who once felt keenly but are now afraid to feel and thereby suffer too much pain or hurt. So they suppress their emotions and stay on a dull or apathethic level much of the time. With these self-suppressed individuals, I try to discover their disturbed musts and show them how to Dispute them. For example, 'I must not let myself really love anyone, for then I could easily get rejected, and I *couldn't* stand that horror!' Or 'I must not feel or express anger because people would hate me, and I would then be a *rotten person*!' Once I help these people to find, Dispute, and surrender these emotion-suppressing ideas, they frequently unleash their suppressed feelings and become more spontaneous and involvable. In RET, of course, we also have many emotion-evocative techniques – such as my famous shame-attacking exercises and my dramatic version of Maxie Maultsby's rational-emotive imagery. These and other RET emotive techniques encourage clients to get in touch with, and often enhance, their feelings.

W.D. In reading your writings it's difficult to get a clear sense of how you vary your therapeutic approach with different clients. We have touched on that issue here and there in this interview, but I wonder if you could give some consideration to the decision rules you might use to lead you to work in different ways with different clients.

A.E. Largely, I assume that most clients widely differ in their goals, values, desires, standards, and personalities but that they are also fairly similar in the musturbatory philosophies that they construct *about* their desires. Their *preferences* are varied and their *tastes* are somewhat unique; but, when they are disturbed, their Jehovian demands that these preferences be met are often amazingly similar. I may very much like coffee, and you may adore tea. But when we are deprived, you will very likely tell yourself, 'I *must* have tea', while I will insist, 'I *must* have coffee'. So, using RET with clients, I *accept* their likes and dislikes but *argue with* their dogmatic commands, demands, musts, shoulds and oughts.

When people are anxious, depressed, self-hating or enraged, they generally have similar ideas, which I can usually guess by finding their Activating Event (*A*) and their emotional-behavioural Consequence (*C*) and then *assuming* what their irrational Beliefs (*B*s) are and *checking* with them to see if I am on the right track. So with most clients, I start with the basic RET processes of uncovering their *B*s and showing them how to scientifically, efficiently and forcefully Dispute them. Normally this works well. But people, because of their different tastes and personalities (which are biologically as well as socially based) may differ widely in their enthusiastic endorsement of or their rigid resistance to RET (and to other kinds of therapy). So I adapt my *teaching* of RET to my clients to their personality-motivated acceptance of and/or resistance to its theory and practice.

W.D. But none the less, you would usually start in the same active, directive and authoritative style that is natural to you?

A.E. I use the usual active-directive RET methods in the first few sessions with the majority of my clients and quite often they begin to improve significantly after from five to ten sessions. When they don't seem to get and begin to use regular RET methods and I see they really are idiosyncratic or resistant, I either become more forceful or I change my pace and start to add something or subtract something to what I usually do. For instance, some clients won't do their homework. I may arrange that they do it during the therapy sessions. Or if they agree to burn money and they don't do their homework and then refrain from burning it, I may burn it for them. Occasionally I refuse to see a recalcitrant client again until *after* she or he has done the agreed-upon homework.

In some cases, I don't have to individualize my general RET approach very much; but in most cases I soon find what works and what doesn't work with specific clients and I emphasize one set of techniques rather than another. Sometimes I even creatively invent new RET variations for especially difficult clients. Yesterday, for example, I was exceptionally gentle with one young woman who said she had been traumatized by her previous therapist's yelling at her, while I was very forceful with another young woman who had seen two cognitive-behaviour therapists who were bright and competent but too weakly confronting.

W.D. Can you give me some more examples of how you adapt your normal therapeutic style?

A.E. Well, let's suppose that clients are really resistant to therapy and particularly to my therapeutic style. Some of them tell me, for example, 'Don't use that vile language', and then I may say, 'I won't use it with you – if I remember!' Or I may make and issue of it and say to them, 'Why can't I use it? I'm not asking *you* to use it. Let's even suppose that I'm wrong about using it. You seem to be upsetting yourself about my wrong behaviour. Now what are you telling yourself to upset yourself about my wrong language?'

Other clients, I find, really have a dire need of approval and they are not going to listen to anything I say unless I give them more approval. So at first I may go out of my way to show them that I really like them and think that they are bright and competent despite their screw-ups. I may deliberately compliment them on the things they do well and forget momentarily about the things they do badly. Later, after gaining good rapport with them, I point out their mistakes and how they can correct them.

With some clients, I find that I make the mistake of thinking they are brighter than they are when actually they are not so bright or are so panicked that they cannot use their intellectual capacities well.

So I switch to showing them how to use rational coping statements instead of RET Disputing – because I can see they are not going to work at Disputing or they are just not able to do the Disputing very well. I try to remember that all therapy, including RET, is as much an art as a science, though I keep trying to make RET more scientific. But teaching, persuading and psychotherapy still depend on the artistic ability of the presenter to reach many different kinds of subjects.

W.D. The process of RET seems to be based on the notion that people can change by weakening their conviction in their irrational Beliefs and strengthening their conviction in their rational Beliefs. However, do you find that clients have different styles or modes of learning which you need to take into account if you are going to adapt RET to their individualistic concerns?

A.E. The answer is Yes. For example, I find that some people had better have a diagram of the *ABC*s of RET to help them understand and use them. So I draw them a diagram and go over it with them.

I have one client right now who is a famous actress and who thinks she knows everything, who rattles on and on during our sessions, and who won't deign to do any Disputing or almost any homework. So I give her strong coping statements to alleviate her anxiety, and that works quite well.

I have other clients who won't do any RET reading. So I tell them to get our audio and video cassettes, and some of them do marvellously with the cassettes, even though they will hardly ever read our pamphlets or books. Some of them tell me, 'I *can't* read; I'm allergic to reading!' I later may show them that they *can* read, but in the meantime get them to record our sessions and to use RET cassettes. So when certain modalities don't work with a client, I change to another modality. Thus, I encourage some clients to come to our four-hour workshops and to my Friday Night Workshops; and they may get more out of this kind of therapy than they do from individual sessions, because they see other people using RET and they learn it more effectively. I urge other clients to join one of my regular therapy groups because they can benefit from group support or use the groups to practise risk-taking self-disclosure.

When any process or technique I employ doesn't seem to be working, I either abandon it or change my method of presenting it. For example, when clients find some RET books too difficult, I give them simpler reading material. Or when they (often foolishly) insist on whining and complaining, I let them go on for a while before I finally show them that they had better look at their underlying irrational philosophies that cause their whining.

W.D. The next issue that I want to raise with you concerns aspects of training; for example, what characteristics do you think in general make a good therapist?

A.E. There are a number of characteristics that I think good therapists had better have, but they are probably all *preferential* rather than *necessary*. So let me list some of these preferences that I often discuss with RET trainees. These include

1 To distinctly enjoy helping people by doing therapy.
2 To be excellent listeners.
3 To be highly intelligent.
4 To be open-minded and flexible – always willing to change their attitudes, manner and methods.
5 To have a clear, workable, therapeutic theory, preferably with outcome studies to back it.
6 To feel and convey to their clients unconditional acceptance.
7 To be creative about adapting old techniques and sometimes inventing new ones.
8 To have a good sense of humour.
9 To keep in mind specific goal-setting for themselves and their clients.
10 To know the therapeutic literature and keep up with new methods.
11 To be secure enough themselves so that they *like* but don't *need* their clients' love and approval.
12 To have high frustration tolerance and patient persistence.
13 To be assertive without being hostile.
14 To honestly check their clients' progress and be ready to change their methods and emphases when thy are not working.
15 To be realistic and not insist that they can help every client all of the time. To be able to accept limited gains.
16 To be good educators and persuaders.
17 To be encouraging and optimistic, but not Pollyanna-ish.
18 To be aware of their own biases and prejudices and sensitive to the cultural, ethnic, religious and other biases of their clients.
19 To endeavour to make therapy as brief as feasible but also to accept the reality that some clients require long-term treatment.

20 To be able and willing to use many different kinds of cognitive, emotive and behavioural techniques and to suitably vary them with different clients.
21 To have a broad background in the biological, social and psychological sciences and keep abreast of new findings in psychophysical areas.
22 To have preferably suffered from and to have overcome some emotional problems themselves and to be able to talk openly to their clients about some of their personal experiences.
23 To be something of an efficiency expert in solving their own and their clients' practical problems of living.
24 To be quite scientific instead of mystical and devout in their outlook toward life.

This list of desirable characteristics for almost any therapist to have may seem quite long, but it is hardly exhaustive. And remember, again, it is a *preferential* rather than a *necessary* list! Also, because many clients have both general and specific problems – are, for example, anxious or depressed about several things but also specifically addicted to smoking, overeating, anorexia, alcohol or drug abuse – and their specific problems may require special therapeutic techniques, a good therapist had better be a generalist but also sometimes specialize in treating special types of clients – and always be ready to refer some special clients to other therapists. Thus I see almost all kinds of clients for individual and group therapy at the psychological clinic at the Institute for Rational-Emotive Therapy in New York. But I often refer my clients with specific problems of vocational choice to one of our other therapists, Dr Diana Richman, who specializes in that area.

W.D. Would you say there are special characteristics which RET therapists need in particular but which perhaps good therapists of other persuasions don't?

A.E. I have a whole list of characteristics that are desirable for RET practitioners to have and that I discuss with our Institute trainees at our supervision sessions. These include

1 To be able to guess what clients' irrational Beliefs (*IB*s) are when the reveal their Activating Events (*A*s) and troublesome Consequences (*C*s); and to be able efficiently to help their clients see these *IB*s and actively Dispute them.
2 To be able to sensibly, vigorously and persuasively Dispute

their clients' irrational Beliefs, convince them to change them, teach them how to regularly do their own Disputing, and see that they steadily keep doing this.

3 To clearly understand the basic theory and practice of RET, to keep up with its new developments, and to continue to use it with themselves and their clients.

4 To fully accept themselves, even when they fail with their clients, and to have high frustration tolerance and patience and persistence in working with difficult clients.

5 To integrate RET with other suitable therapy methods and to be flexible enough to use anti-RET methods at times with clients who can't or won't effectively employ RET.

6 To use empirical and realistic Disputations of their clients' self-defeating inferences and attributions; but also to look for the underlying absolutist shoulds and musts behind their attributions and reveal this to the clients and teach them how to find and actively Dispute them, too.

7 To try to help as many clients as possible to achieve a profound philosophic change, but not to insist that they all achieve it.

8 To get feedback from their clients as to *how* these clients feel about them as therapists and how they think RET is working, and to use this feedback to improve their therapy.

9 To have a good grasp of the philosophy of science and to use it in their Disputation and in teaching clients how to Dispute their *IB*s.

10 To have a humanistic and existential outlook and to incorporate it into RET therapy.

11 To use RET in his or her own life and to become more rational and self-helping as he or she continues to use it.

12 To strive to be a forceful, vigorous, encouraging RET practitioner while at the same time always trying to be open-minded about clients, about the world, and about RET itself.

13 To be exceptionally experimental as a person and as a therapist.

14 To be thoroughly accepting of their clients but not of some of the clients' behaviours, and to endeavour to teach their clients to fully accept themselves, but to carefully evaluate what they do.

W.D. And some of these are characteristics you look for in people who apply for RET training?

A.E. Yes – or at least I look for their potential to achieve these characteristics.

W.D. One of the interesting issues in the field of training is the role of personal therapy in training novice therapists. What's your view of the role of personal therapy in training?

A.E. Well, I take the same view as Carl Rogers did, that it's *desirable* but not *necessary* for therapists to have personal psychotherapy. Because I have found some very good RET therapists who have never had therapy themselves. I think they had self-therapy – they read the RET literature and used its principles on themselves. But they never had any formal therapy.

W.D. Suppose an RET therapist came to you and said, 'Look, I don't have any emotional problems at the moment but I would like an opportunity to explore various facets of my personality and different aspects of my life, to look at my values and goals so that I can find out whether or not I am living my life effectively.' Would you recommend that they see an RET therapist, or are there other therapies which may help them more in that particular quest?

A.E. Well, I think that most other therapies have so many disadvantages that I practically never recommend them. Another form of therapy, like psychoanalysis, may help people to explore themselves, but it almost always gives them all kinds of misleading experiences and ideas as well. I might well recommend an RET therapist but not another form of therapy. Or I might work with them on self-exploration myself, and in the course of it I would show them some of the irrational ideas they probably have, even though they may not think they do. But I believe that most therapies, aside from behaviour therapy and cognitive-behaviour therapy, are iatrogenic – they often do more harm than good. And even when they help, they are usually too long-winded and inefficient.

W.D. So you are saying that RET is not only good for helping people over their disturbances but also for encouraging them to explore themselves?

A.E. Right – if they just want to do that. But I don't think that people often just want to explore themselves or they wouldn't come to therapy.

W.D. They might not call it therapy, they might call it personal exploration or personal growth counselling.

A.E. That's all right, but I am prejudiced enough to believe that RET can do better with personal growth counselling than the other kinds of therapies.

W.D. What stance would you take if it did actually appear that the client didn't have too many irrational ideas blocking them but really did want to do a wide-ranging exploration?

A.E. Then I would help them explore how they can actualize themselves, just as I do with ordinary clients who first benefit from RET by minimizing their disturbances and then go on to the next step: 'Could you do better, could you enjoy yourself *more*? Let's discuss your goals, purposes and ideals and see how you could get more pleasure, more joy out of life, without screwing yourself.'

W.D. But it sounds as if you would be sceptical that such a person wouldn't have some musts or irrational ideas lurking somewhere.

A.E. Yes, I would be very sceptical, because practically all people have them! Even RET practitioners, including myself, who work hard to minimize their dogmatic musts, keep recreating some of them for the rest of their lives. That seems to be the human condition – to have strong desires, and to fairly frequently transmute them into Jehovian musts.

W.D. Supervision seems to play quite an important part in the training of RET therapists. Do you suggest that experienced RET therapists have regular ongoing supervision?

A.E. It would be better if from time to time they asked some of our senior therapists to go over some of their tapes. Not all the time, but every once in a while, so that they would have continuing supervision. That would be preferable.

W.D. How about yourself? Do you ever send a tape out to somebody for a second opinion or check?

A.E. I don't recall the last time I did that, and I may well be wrong in not doing it. But I often play some of my more unusual tapes for our therapists here, to show them some of the things I do, and I get some valuable comments back. I also frequently describe aspects of what I am doing with my clients to my supervisees and see how they feel about my methods.

W.D. So you suggest a periodic supervisory relationship between recently trained and more experienced RET therapists. You don't seem to be recommending very frequent ongoing supervision for those people, though.

A.E. Not if they seem to be doing well and are not getting into any difficulty, and it looks as if they are doing the therapy effectively. But I would still recommend occasional supervision. I also recommend that they come to advanced workshops and think tanks on RET that the Institute arranges from time to time.

W.D. Now, what attitude do you have on the issue of brief therapy?

A.E. My contention is that with many clients, especially the neurotic ones, RET is essentially a brief, or a brief*er*, therapy in comparison with other therapies. I originated RET because of the inefficiency of psychoanalysis and the interminability of the psychoanalytic process. Psychoanalysis, even psychoanalytically oriented psychotherapy, tends to go on for years getting at the so-called basic repressed feelings and ideas of the client. When I was a practising analyst, I found out that this was largely an unnecessary waste of time.

The goal of RET with clients is to determine what their underlying irrational philosophies and basic self-defeating behaviours are, to reveal this to them as soon as feasible, and to encourage them quickly to start working to change their dysfunctional thoughts, feelings and actions. Ideally, as I noted before, I would like to have them make a profound philosophical change and effectuate what RET calls the elegant solution for their problems. This includes (1) to eliminate the symptoms for which the clients came to therapy; (2) to maintain their symptom removal; (3) to extend their gains to other kinds of anxiety, self-hating or depression than they originally talked about in therapy; (4) to keep working on acquiring anti-musturbatory philosophies and appropriate feelings and behaviours until they reach a point where they rarely become anxious, depressed or enraged again – not never, but rarely; and (5) to be so RET-oriented that, when they do fall back to dysfunctional feelings and behaviours, they can quickly zero in on them and see what they are telling themselves to create these disturbances and quickly overcome them again by actively Disputing their underlying irrational Beliefs. They then, as the years go by, tend to become automatically more rational and self-helping. That is the *elegant* RET solution.

Though ideally we would try to get everybody to that point, RET recognizes that many clients will never make it. Many will benefit from an inelegant solution, will improve significantly and get rid of their symptoms, but will never get to the point where they rarely needlessly upset themselves again.

I try to get all my clients, as quickly as we can, to this kind of better, more elegant solution and not to let therapy go on interminably. After a while, a few months, six months or a year, most of them realize that they are much better than they were before and are upsetting themselves less often. So we agree to change the sessions to every other week, every third week or even less. Finally, usually in less than a year, my clients stop having regular sessions. Some of them come back occasionally for booster shots and some I never see again as clients, although they may keep coming to my Friday Night Workshops or other Institute workshops. When they are in touch, I often see that they keep using the RET techniques over the years.

If RET is properly done, it usually takes a lot less time, with fewer sessions, than most other therapies. I see many of my clients for a whole year, which is a reasonable length of time, but they tend to have only twenty or twenty-five sessions during this period. RET is one of the few therapies that was originally *designed* to be brief, though psychoanalysis has brief forms and some of the other therapies have brief adaptations.

Brief therapy, however, often doesn't work with borderline clients, especially with those I call the borderline-pluses; and some psychotics and other seriously aberrated people can benefit from it almost forever. They don't necessarily need it perpetually once every week, but they benefit from fairly steady therapy for a long time because they require help for practical problems and for leading a fuller existence, and some of them had better have considerable help all their lives. I see some semi-psychotic and psychotic individuals for ten or more years, but after a while only see them a few times each year.

W.D. You consider yourself to be a promulgator of RET and it seems as if one of your major life goals is to make the message of RET as widely available as possible. Is that correct?

A.E. That's definitely so. I aim to keep giving it to therapists and to the public through articles, books, cassettes, lectures, workshops and other kinds of presentations. When it is found wanting. I try to polish it up and revise it. One of the reasons why I do so much therapy, and see as many as 140 people each week in my individual and group therapy sessions, is to keep polishing RET theory and practice, adding to and subtracting from it. So my therapy clients are my main laboratory for doing that. I also keep reading a great deal of the literature on therapy; and I and the Institute keep sponsoring and doing research on RET.

W.D. The point has often been made, sometimes jokingly and sometimes seriously, about the repetitive nature of your writings. It's been said that you really have only one book but you have written it fifty or sixty times. How valid do you think that criticism is?

A.E. Well, it's partly invalid. The person who said it recently was Larry Beutler on a panel. While I was being introduced and the introducer said, 'Albert Ellis has written over fifty books', Beutler said jokingly that I written the same book fifty times. Part of what he said is, of course, false – because he forgot that about twenty of my books are about sex, love and marriage and may have some RET in them but had all kinds of other material in them as well. Some of them were written before I even started RET, like *The Folklore of Sex* (Ellis 1951) and *The American Sexual Tragedy* (Ellis 1954). I've written a score of books on self-help for the public, and another score of books for therapists to show them how to do RET. They overlap to some degree, but they are rather different kinds of books. My self-help and my professional books on RET have the same theory but hardly the same practice. Several of my books describe the application of RET to different areas – for example, my book on *Executive Leadership* (Ellis 1972c) applies it to executives, and that's hardly the same as applying it to sex and marriage or to general anxiety. I did one book, *The Psychology of Sex Offenders* (Ellis and Brancale 1956), that is a research study, and that has no RET in it, and another book, *Murder and Assassination* (Ellis and Gullo 1971), that is also largely a research study. So the allegation that I've written one book fifty times is hardly true!

W.D. But even if it were true to a large extent, it seems to me that you wouldn't be concerned too much because if you are a promulgator, the more books you write the more chances you have of these books being read by a large number of people.

A.E. That's right. Publishers often ask me for a book using a somewhat different application of RET that is not included in my other books. So I will do the one they ask for, even though it overlaps with my previous books. Your book, for example, *The Essential Albert Ellis* (Dryden 1990), of course includes my previous writings. But I wanted to see it in print because it revives some of my old essays and puts them in book form.

W.D. Isn't there a danger in being a promulgator that it's easy to push the positives of RET? To give you credit, you do recognize and admit criticisms when they are pointed out to you, but you don't spontaneously bring them up. Isn't there a danger that in the quest for spreading your ideas to the the widest range of people there may be a tendency to edit out the negatives?

A.E. I am sure that is a danger, and I would say it's a danger for practically all theorists and outstanding therapists, such as Sigmund Freud. Wilhelm Reich and Fritz Perls. We all push what we think are the good points of our therapy and only when people raise the bad points do we bother to answer them. I think I've answered more of my critics than almost anybody else has because I have published over a score of articles giving direct answers to their objections. I don't think Sigmund Freud and other therapists did so as often. They frequently gave indirect answers or they ignored their critics completely. But we all tend to give a one-sided view of the practices we favour, and I often do it, too. That's what a propagandist and a promulgator will do.

W.D. Now as you look back over your career as an RET therapist, theorist and promulgator, does one book stand out for you as having given you the greatest satisfaction?

A.E. The books I think of as giving me the most satisfaction because they actually keep in print and still get referred to over the years are certainly, for the public, *How to Live with a Neurotic* (Ellis 1975), and the original *A Guide to Rational Living* (Ellis and Harper 1961), which is now *A New Guide to Rational Living* (Ellis and Harper 1975) and has sold about a million and a half copies over the years. *Humanistic Psychotherapy* (Ellis 1973a) is sort of in that class because the public still reads and benefits a good deal from it. *A Guide to Personal Happiness* (Ellis and Becker 1982) has been in print since 1982 and has sold a lot of copies. I also think my new book, *How to Stubbornly Refuse to Make Yourself Miserable about Anything – Yes, Anything!* (Ellis 1988) will continue over the years. I may revise these books, but they go on year after year. My book on anger (Ellis 1977a) was just recently put out for the first time in Australia, for example, and I just learned that it quickly sold out a large first edition.

W.D. But just let me push you to name one book, because I did ask for one and you came out with about half a dozen! If you really had to choose the one book which gives you the most satisfaction and pleasure, what would it be?

A.E. Well, I'm not sure! Let's go to the professional books, which incidentally are also read by the public. To my surprise, a good number of my clients have told me that one book which helped them more than any other book, although I didn't write it for that purpose, was *Reason and Emotion in Psychotherapy* (Ellis 1962). That's been cited professionally more than any of my other books. But I think it's cited by people who have never read it, because they know that it's a seminal book and they cite it as a main reference. Who knows whether they ever actually read the goddamn book! So that's given me a good deal of satisfaction as a professional book. Then *Humanistic Psychotherapy* (Ellis 1973a) was really written largely for the professional field and is often cited, and is one of my favourites. One of the very best, to my way of thinking, is a book I did with you, *The Practice of Rational-Emotive Therapy* (Ellis and Dryden 1987). I especially like this one because the first few chapters bring RET practice and theory up to date.

In many respects, my favourite among my books is my little-known volume, *Is Objectivism a Religion?* (Ellis 1968), in which I show how dogmatic and devout, and in many ways irrational, was Ayn Rand. A number of readers who know her philosophy have heartily congratulated me on criticizing it in depth. I agree that I did a good job!

W.D. Is there one piece of work with a client that has given you the most pleasure?

A.E. I remember the work with one of my borderline clients, in the 1970s, because it helped me to clarify the theory of and practical approach to discomfort anxiety and low frustration tolerance. Other clients certainly helped me to develop other theories and practices. But I have seen so many thousands of clients over the years that it is hard to recall outstanding cases.

W.D. Well, let's go to the other side of the coin. As you look back over your career, which are the things you most regret about your work as an RET therapist?

A.E. One of the things that I probably regret more than anything else is my original use of the term 'Rational Therapy', which I later changed to Rational-Emotive Therapy. Ray Corsini keeps after me to change the name to Rational-Emotive Behavioural Therapy (REBT) and he may well be right about that because that's what it more accurately is. Actually, if I had called it at the start Cognitive-Emotive Behavioural Therapy that might have even been better, because people still don't like the word 'rational'. Many therapists tend to favour the word 'cognitive' rather than 'rational'. RET was, in fact, the original cognitive-emotive behavioural therapy, and I think calling it rational-emotive therapy has turned off a lot of therapists who hate the word 'rational' and give it all kinds of connotations that are inaccurate. I couldn't have foreseen this when I first used to term 'rational therapy', but with hindsight I now see that it was probably wrong. I'm glad I changed it to Rational-Emotive Therapy but probably that wasn't enough, and I still may follow Ray's advice and change it to rational-emotive-behavioural therapy.

W.D. Any other regrets?

A.E. My other regret is that RET, unlike Beck's cognitive therapy, has not yet had a manual (though we are currently working on one), and consequently it has led to less research than it otherwise would have generated. Beck had a fairly clear-cut manual from 1978 onward and that has encouraged research into cognitive therapy rather than research into RET, so I think we were mistaken not to write a clear-cut manual earlier, which we certainly could have done.

W.D. You mentioned several of your books as having given you a lot of satisfaction – can you think of any of your publications that you are unhappy with and wish you hadn't written or hadn't published?

A.E. One that was really very badly done, but that I was sort of forced to push through at the last minute, was my book on *Nymphomania* (Ellis and Sagarin 1967). The publisher rewrote parts of this book without my real consent. Then I found some small print in the contract saying they had a right to do this and it was a choice between letting them do it or not having the book published at all. So I thought it was better to have it published, though I was unenthusiastic about their rewriting. Even with *Humanistic Psychotherapy* (Ellis 1973a), a good book, I was going to change it around and make various alterations but the publishers said they had already got it accepted by one of the big book clubs and there was no time for me to revise it. So some of my books were rushed through the press and although they are basically OK, I regretted their being published too quickly because they were by no means as good as they could have been. I also had to force Prentice-Hall into putting out a new edition of *A Guide to Rational Living*, because the old edition was still selling very well and they didn't want to revise it. So I threatened to write a letter to the *American Psychologist* describing how they had resisted my updating this work and pointed out that as they publish so many psychological books that this would give them a bad name among psychologists. So they finally brought out a new edition!

W.D. Now as you look towards your own personal future in terms of the development of RET, do you see yourself going on pretty much as you are now, seeing the numbers of clients you see now, going around doing workshops and writing, or do you predict that your role might change?

A.E. Well, assuming that my health and energies continue until my death – which seems unlikely – I expect to die in harness and not to curb the number of clients and groups, or my workshops and talks, or my writing. Now if my energy level goes down or I get some serious ailment, I will have to curb some activities but I can't say which ones. But I intend, if I can, to keep busy with various aspects of RET till the day I die, and I hope that will be at least in my late nineties!

W.D. After you shuffle off this mortal – but rational – coil, do you think it would be healthy or unhealthy for the future of RET to have a figurehead to replace you?

A.E. If there were a good figurehead then it would be healthy. For example, in the case of Alfred Adler, he was succeeded by a very good figurehead, Rudolf Dreikurs, who is still respected and who gave his name to the Rudolf Dreikurs Institute in Chicago. That's fine. If somebody can really take my place at the head RET – you, or Ray DiGiuseppe, or Janet Wolfe, or Michael Bernard, or some other outstanding RETer – that would be great. But there may be nobody of that calibre willing to devote the time and energy to fill that role. If there is and they can carry on sanely and passionately, and continue to change and add to RET – that would be fine!

W.D. Now as you look to the future of RET, if you were to make a prediction, where do you think it's likely to go in the future?

A.E. Well, my guess is that RET – whether it's called RET or not – has already infiltrated general psychotherapy and cognitive-behaviour therapy, in particular, and will keep doing so in the future. The theory and practice of RET will find its way into a large part of general psychotherapy, just as some aspects of psychoanalysis are already co-terminous today with the whole psychotherapeutic field. I hope, naturally, that RET, cognitive-behaviour therapy and its derivatives, will increasingly prevail, and that's what I would predict. Some aspects of it may be changed or abandoned. But especially in the area of psycho-educational interventions and self-help materials, I predict that much of the theory and practice of RET will be increasingly used in schools, in the work-place, in the mass media, and in other public presentations.

W.D. Are you optimistic about the future of psychotherapy in general?

A.E. Well, I take an optimistic view in believing that general psychotherapy will include more and more RET and will, I hope, eliminate some of the worst aspects of current practice. But I also hope that more RET will be incorporated into areas like stress management and family counselling. There are now trainers in business who use all kinds of techniques, often largely encounter exercises, and I think they will increasingly incorporate aspects of RET into their work. Again, I think that education will become more psychotherapeutic and then be RET-oriented. So I am optimistic about that.

W.D. Do you have any concerns about the future of psychotherapy in general?

A.E. It could easily go in a direction opposite to RET and incorporate various therapies that are in my opinion anti-therapeutic (see Chapter 4). However, although there may be new fads, the field, I think, will return to some of the basic principles of RET because they will probably be shown to work better for most of the people most of the time than most of the other therapies. For example, right now transpersonal, mystical and New Age therapies, which often induce people to rely on magical forces rather than on their own abilities to change, have become very popular. I hope this is a fad and will fade. But people are often so basically irrational about themselves and about the kinds of therapies they choose that anti-scientific therapies may keep thriving. Too bad – but not *awful*!

W.D. Finally, on this subject, what is your own assessment about your own contribution to the field of psychotherapy? How would you like to be remembered?

A.E. Well, I would like to be remembered truthfully as the father or grandfather, if you like, of cognitive-behaviour therapy. I certainly am not the father of cognitive therapy, because I largely derived it from philosophers – especially Epicurus, Epictetus and Immanuel Kant – and earlier psychotherapists – including Pierre Janet and Alfred Adler, who were also cognitivists. As for behaviour therapy, Watson, Skinner and Eysenck preceded me and I learned much from them. But I think that I was the first definite clear-cut cognitive-behavioural therapist. There were others who used something close to it but they were much more behavioural *or* cognitive and hardly emotive at all. The *popularity* of cognitive-behaviour and rational-emotive therapy largely came though my teaching. The fine work of Albert Bandura, Donald Meichenbaum, Aaron Beck, William Glasser, Richard Lazarus, Arnold Lazarus, and other well-known cognitive behaviourists started in the 1960s, a decade after I began widely promulgating RET in 1955. Most probably, they all were heavily influenced by me, though some of them, like Glasser, sometimes deny this. So most therapists and theorists acknowledge that I was the originator of cognitive-behaviour therapy and some don't, but that is how I would like to be remembered.

W.D. But in your own words, it wouldn't be terrible if you weren't?

A.E. No! If I'm never mentioned in human history but cognitive-behaviour therapy goes on, that's not *OK* but I can live with it – and not make myself miserable about my lack of recognition. I do, however, greatly enjoy the present popularity of RET and cognitive-behaviour therapy and hope that they continue to grow and develop.

4 VIEWS ON OTHER THERAPIES

WINDY DRYDEN Now, Al, I want to discuss your views on other approaches to psychotherapy. The way I want to do this is to look at the major traditions in psychotherapy as well as some more current approaches which fall outside these. First I would like to ask you about your views on psychoanalysis and its more current derivatives like briefer psychoanalytically oriented therapy and the like. What are you most against *vis-à-vis* the psychoanalytic tradition in psychotherapy?

ALBERT ELLIS Well, I object to most of its basic theories – not all of them – especially the view that our disturbances are created by our past history. Not only do the Freudians believe this, but the object relations people strongly believe it, too. According to the Freudians, the object relations and the psychoanalytic self theorists (such as Kohut and Kernberg), if your mother looks at you cross-eyed in the first year or two, that sets the stage for your hating yourself and even for your becoming borderline or psychotic. I don't think people get too upset in the first few years of life, unless they are born with strong borderline, psychotic or organic tendencies. From their second or third year onward, especially when they develop language and internal thinking, they *then* often change their desires to demands, insist that their mothers, fathers, and others absolutely *must* treat them as they command, and often – indeed, probably, usually – start *making* themselves neurotic – yes, start *constructing* their grandiose demands on themselves, on their parents, on others, and on the world. When they are criticized, neglected or abused, they usually are *more* desiring (which is healthy) and *more* demanding (which is neurotic) that external conditions be better than they are.

But even if they were raised ideally, and never neglected or abused, most of them seem to have a strong inborn tendency to be perfectionistic, to down themselves when they perform poorly or are disapproved, and to damn others and the world when they are treated less ideally than they presumably *must* be treated. Being innate, neurotic demanders and commanders (as well as healthy wishers and preferers), they *bring* their grandiose philosophy *to* their parents and others; and because they rarely are treated as ideally as they assumedly *should* be, they frequently *make* themselves disturbed – and then, of course, *put* the blame for their disturbed feelings *on to* their parents and their environment. Psychoanalysts, orthodox behaviour therapists, and most other (than RET) therapists think unscientifically, pretty much as little children do, and falsely believe that because children's poor parental rearing and environmental conditions *contribute* to their disturbance (at point *A*, Activating Events) that they also *cause* this disturbance (at point *C*, emotional Consequence). RET tries to correct this faulty thinking by placing the main (though not the only) contribution or 'cause' at point *B* – the children's Belief system. Where psychoanalysis (and radical behaviourism) say that children are largely *made* neurotic by their early rearers, RET holds that they mainly *construct* their neuroses by taking the standards, preferences and values that they (gullibly) take from their parents and culture, and foolishly *adding* to them their own Jehovanistic musts and demands.

After falsely holding that children and adults *get* upset by their environment, psychoanalysis is largely anti-philosophic and misses the extremely important point that humans are born philosophers and that it's mainly their philosophies, especially their imperative and absolutist musts, that upset them rather than their so-called experiences. The term *experience* really hides a great deal of philosophy, because experience consists of what is happening to you *plus* your philosophy, your attitudes and ideas, *about* what is happening (and about what you often *make* happen). So psychoanalysts, and many other therapists, are so hung up on your *experiences* with the analyst and in your outside life that they often fail to look at the equally or more important things you *tell yourself* about these experiences. Most experiential therapy also tends to follow this poor psychoanalytic lead.

Psychoanalysis tends to give superficial explanations of what goes on in people's lives and explains it in terms of events and happenings. For example if a woman has difficulty in finding a mate, they say that is because she has a *pattern* of picking the wrong men that explains why she avoids or rejects better ones. Her *pattern*, they then say, was set in her early childhood, presumably as a result of her special relationships with her father or brothers. But this *pattern* explanation doesn't discover what she did to *create* the pattern! Actually if the pattern really exists – and you can be sure that her analyst willy-nilly will convince her that it does, whether or not she actually follows it! – the pattern was *devised* by her specific thoughts, feelings, attitudes and philosophies she *constructed* about the early and later events of her life; and by *acting* on her own preferential and musturbatory *Beliefs*, she *made* the pattern habitual. So when her analyst describes her behaviour as a pattern, and she agrees, 'Oh yes, that's right, it's my pattern', neither she nor her therapist really see the important cognitive-emotive specifics of how she, and *not* her environment, *created* the pattern, nor do they understand what she had better *think*, *feel* and *do* to give up this pattern and construct a more useful life.

Psychoanalysis is probably *the* most wasteful form of therapy ever invented, because it encourages clients to continue in treatment for years and years and to focus on long-winded and side-tracking free associations, dream analysis and exploration of the past. So it is probably the *most* inefficient form of therapy ever invented, even when it helps somewhat. The reason I gave it up was largely because it was inefficient and wasteful. Very often it is iatrogenic because the analyst foists on you problems that you never really had or have – such as your wanting to fuck your mother or father. Innumerable people – especially bright ones – drop out of psychoanalysis because they soon see that it is not helpful and that, instead, it does more harm than good.

Psychoanalysis also leads to dependency more than perhaps any other form of therapy. Clients come to depend on two, three, four or five days a week with their analyst, and on discussing everything they think and do with him or her before they decide what to think, feel and do themselves. Although analysts are supposed to mainly listen and are not supposed to give advice, they almost always do. So clients get dependent on the analyst instead of depending on their own Disputing and their own self-help methods that we invariably emphasize in RET.

Psychoanalysis also includes many overgeneralizations that are foisted on its clients. It falsely teaches them, for instance, that *all* people have an Oedipus or Electra complex, or that *all* people become neurotic because of their early object relations with their parents and other family members. Analysts rarely acknowledge the exceptions to their rigid rule; they vastly overgeneralize about human nature and emotional disturbance, and that is why Bertrand Russell, Karl Popper, and other leading philosophers of science have found psychoanalysis to be largely anti-scientific.

W.D. Well, I guess that somebody who was psychoanalytically inclined might say that you are equally dogmatic and overgeneralizing when you claim that people who are distressed *all* have irrational Beliefs.

A.E. No, that is not quite so. First of all, RET says that *most* neurotics – not *all* – disturb themselves by constructing irrational, dogmatic *musts* about their usually healthy *preferences*. Second, it states this in testable falsifiable hypotheses, while some of the main psychoanalytic theories – about the ego and the id, for example – are so vague and overgeneral that it is virtually impossible to test them empirically and to falsify them. Third, RET doesn't say, as many analysts unfortunately do, that borderline, psychotic, organically impaired, and other seriously disturbed people are psychologically warped by their early experiences, while RET holds that almost all such individuals have a biological as well as psychological disturbance and that therefore they often had better be treated with medication.

Psychoanalysts, especially Freudians, often stick to the dogma – which has considerable evidence against it – that just about all people first go through the oral, then the anal, and then the genital stage of development and that they later on in childhood undergo a latency period. As a sexologist for almost fifty years, I can practically assure you that innumerable people do *not* go through these regular sequences, and that even those who do at first have *sensual* feelings that Freud often confused with *sexual* feelings. Because Freud found (or invented!) a few cases of the Oedipus complex, psychoanalysis often still holds that practically *everybody* has an Oedipus complex. And because a few people really do act towards the analyst as they did towards their father or mother, psychonanalysis claims that *all* clients undergo a pronounced transference relationship. Analysts who overgeneralize in this way are quite unscientific.

Psychoanalysts also dogmatically believe in deeply unconscious or repressed thoughts and feelings instead of the more credible view that many of our thoughts and bodily processes are automatic or preconscious but that few of them are deeply unconscious or repressed. RET assumes that many, perhaps most, of our disturbing thoughts – our rigid shoulds, oughts, musts, demand and commands – are by no means at our full conscious awareness, but instead are just below the level of consciousness and can fairly easily be inferred, looked for, and clearly brought to consciousness. If we assume that we have them (on the grounds of RET theory), if we actively look for them, and if we check the evidence for and against our having them we can usually find them fairly easily. Once we do, it is not difficult to bring them to consciousness again whenever we use them to upset ourselves. While psychoanalysis often takes a number of years to supposedly get people to unrepress their 'deeply' unconscious thoughts and feelings, RET shows people how to find their tacit, implicit and unconscious disturbing thoughts in only a few sessions; and it simultaneously, and more importantly, shows them how to start *revising* their irrational demands and how to change them back into sensible preferences.

Psychoanalysts rarely give therapeutic homework. Freud occasionally gave it – with good results! But it's really not part of psychoanalysis to give specific homework assignments. Analysts ignore RET's Insight no. 3: No matter how clearly you see how you originally upset yourself and how you are still holding on to neurotic musturbatory philosophies today, there's usually no way but work and practice – yes, *work and practice* – to change your self-defeating thoughts, feelings and actions.

W.D. Well, they have the working-through stage of therapy.

A.E. Yes, but what does working through consist of? Mainly, working through consists of cognitive changes, or you work through the transference relationship with your analyst, or you fully accept that you hated your mother and still do. It rarely consists of the specific agreed-upon homework that is commonly employed in RET and cognitive-behavioural therapy (CBT).

I said in the early 1970s, and I still do, that most of the analytic techniques (especially the Harry Stack Sullivan relationship and the Freudian transference methods) may help some people to *feel* better but not to *get* better, because they rarely help them make a basic philosophic change (Ellis 1972b).

Especially with catharsis, you go for session after session and tell the analyst what a louse your mother is and what a louse your husband is, and after every session you may feel a lot better but that's very far from getting better! Again, if your problem is dependency – which a great many clients have – very frequently that problem is exacerbated by your relationship with your analyst; and any Disputing he or she does – because analysts do do some Disputing, they bring in a little realism sooner or later – is low-level Disputing.

W.D. What do you mean by low-level Disputing?

A.E. Well, first of all, it is only empirical. Thus, you say to your analyst, 'My husband always hates me', and the analyst may Dispute that and ask, 'Is it true that he *always* hates you?' Or you may report, 'My child always says this', or 'My child is against me', 'My child is deliberately plaguing me', and in many cases the analyst will confront you with reality and show you that you are probably exaggerating. But this is low-level Disputing. Analysts will rarely confront you with your basic philosophy, your underlying perfectionism, or your musturbatory irrational Beliefs – unless they have incorporated some RET techniques, as I think that many are doing today. They often use many non-analytic or anti-psychoanalytic methods and then when their therapy works they falsely say that it's due to the analytic process.

Psychoanalysts don't really have many good emotive-evocative techniques, except the so-called transference relationship between them and their clients. They don't have exercises, such as the famous RET shame-attacking exercises; and they don't really have fables, stories and analogies, though some of them throw them in. Years ago, an analyst in Chicago used a lot of humour; but Lawrence Kubie wrote a famous paper saying don't ever be humorous because that means you are being sarcastic and negative and people will take offence! So analysts don't devise special emotive-evocative techniques, which is probably why psychodrama and Gestalt therapy became so popular, because they do include many dramatic exercises.

W.D. Do you consider that psychoanalytic approaches have any advantages in terms of therapeutic value? You obviously have a lot of critical things to say about their disadvantages, but in terms of reframing are there any good sides?

A.E. Yes, there are at least two major good things about psychoanalysis. One is the theory of psychodynamics, that when you do something dysfunctional it may not be a result of deep repression of your unconscious intentions, as the analysts usually claim; but it may arise from your preconscious or lightly underlying motives. Thus, you may be nice to your mother not just because you love her but because you direly need her love, which you may not fully recognize. Or you may hate her, not because she acted cruelly to you (as you falsely claim that she did), but because she didn't baby you as you think she *should* have done. So when the analyst finds your underlying motivations, it gives you an explanation for what you're doing – a truer explanation than the one you had before. So analysis can very often give you interesting insights. In RET we often use psychodynamic explanations but we do not run them into the ground and invent 'deeply unconscious' explanations for your behaviour that are often false and then cram them down your throat. Some day I'm going to write a paper on how psychodynamics are used in RET.

Second, Freud and his daughter, Anna, nicely described human defences, even though they exaggerated somewhat and created projections and reaction formations that are often more poetry than truth. Psychoanalysts say that when you do something, your reasons for your actions may really be defensive. Thus, when you're caught with your hand in the cookie jar, you rationalize and claim, 'The cookies just happened to fall into my hand'.

Analysts often 'find' these defences when they don't really exist. But by and large, humans *are* defensive, as I show in *How to Live with a Neurotic* (Ellis 1957; 1975). I describe a whole series of defences in that book. That part of analytic theory is good, but analysts never really show you how to minimize your self-defeating defensiveness. They say that if you show people their defences, they get insight into them and presumably give them up. But that's not so. Using RET, we show people how they are blaming *themselves*, not merely their *behaviour*, and therefore need defences to ward off their self-castigation. We help them to rid themselves of the blame underneath that spurs them to create defences. This concept of the defence system, which psychoanalytic theory was the first to recognize, adds a lot to therapeutic technique and understanding. Analysts also have several other theories, such as the interpersonal relations theories of Harry Stack Sullivan, that are useful.

W.D. Let's move on now to your views about humanistic therapies.

A.E. There are two kinds of humanism. First, the beneficial humanism promoted by the American Humanistic Association (AHA) that includes therapeutic humanism where you study the person as a whole, you promote self-actualization, you view people as non-mechanical, as responsible for their own feelings and behaviours. This kind of humanism promotes peaceful human relationships, favours both individualism and social interest, fosters choice rather than determinism, aims for openness and flexibility. But then there is the dubious kind of humanism which the Association for Humanistic Psychology (AHP) often favours. This brand emphasizes sensory rather than cognitive processes, overstresses bodily approaches to psychotherapy, is frequently anti-intellectual, and is very often mystical, transcendental, cultish and anti-scientific.

W.D. Let's just take a couple of those. What are your specific criticisms about the sensory and bodily approaches?

A.E. That they have their good points but are overdone. They mostly help you feel better but not get better. Some of the body exercises, such as the sensual and sexual ones, are really risk-taking and shame-taking exercises, so they may help uptight people loosen up. Others, like the martial arts, include self-discipline and rational thinking. Massage, Yoga and dance therapy are enjoyable enough but mainly consist, from a therapeutic standpoint, of cognitive distraction, may increase short-range rather than long range hedonism, and often distract people from making a profound, philosophic change.

Some of the physical therapies stem from Wilhelm Reich, who foolishly thought that if a therapist shows clients how to get a perfect orgasm, that will release their body armouring, free all their bottled-up emotions, drive away their physical diseases (including cancer!), and make them perfectly sane and undisturbed. Lots of luck!

W.D. Couldn't some of these physical techniques lead to cognitive changes?

A.E. Oh yes, they definitely could. Because, for example, when you use the Feldenkrais or other physical posturing methods and you change your posture, you can tell yourself, 'Look, I can change. I can behave differently. I can control my own destiny.' You then change cognitively as well as physically, and that sometimes helps you emotionally.

W.D. One of the hypotheses of re-evaluation co-counselling is that you are more likely to make a cognitive change after you have had an opportunity to disclose what you are concerned about in your life and to do it in a cathartic manner.

A.E. But that's abreaction, not physical methodology. There is no question that some people change when they let out their feelings, as well as when they exercise or do other physical things. The exercise – like jogging – may even help them think more clearly. But largely, my guess is that what people tell themselves about catharsis, abreaction and physical exercises affect their feelings and, especially, their disturbances more than do the exercises themselves.

W.D. Let's specifically look at one or two of the more popular approaches to humanistic psychology. Let's start with person-centred therapy. What do you think are the advantages and disadvantages of person-centred therapy?

A.E. Well, person-centred therapy was developed by Carl Rogers and its big advantage is that you show people they are able to accept themselves fully – the principle of unconditional positive regard. I don't think person-centred therapists do it effectively, because they do it mainly by giving the client *conditional* positive regard. Thus, if Rogers or one of his disciples fully accepts you when you view yourself as a worm, you then say to yourself, 'Great! If Rogers accepts me unconditionally, I must be a good person!' But then you haven't learned how to *un*conditionally accept yourself – *with or without* Rogers' acceptance.

But Rogerian therapy may help people see that they are persons in their own right and that they have a right to be happy and to actualize themselves; moreover, they don't necessarily have to do so through achievement. On the other hand, Rogerians may help clients rid themselves of their achievement need but it often reinforces their dire need for love. Rogerians give clients approval and acceptance, care for them; and then the clients often think that they *must* have this kind of caring – and become *more* disturbed!

But person-centred therapy does include the view that you are responsible for yourself, that you had better be socially concerned, that you can change, and that you have growth potential. So to a large degree it does have a therapeutic philosophy. The disadvantages are that it works mainly through modelling and caring, rather than by actively teaching people how to think for themselves, and therefore, as I noted above, leads to conditional and not *un*conditional self-acceptance.

W.D. Why would you call it conditional?

A.E. The usual illustration I give is that in the old days, in the 1940s or 1950s, you would go to see Carl Rogers and say, 'I hate myself!' and he would say to you, reflecting your feelings, 'Oh, you really hate yourself? You really feel like killing yourself, don't you?' So you might well go out and kill yourself! But then Carl changed. In the 1970s and 1980s you would say to him, 'I hate myself. I'm doing these rotten things and I am a rotten person!' Carl would then respond, 'But I think you're OK. I think you're a nice person. Yes, you do those rotten things, but I can still accept you.' He never would say, 'Now, look, let me show you how to accept yourself *even* if you continue to do rotten things – and *even* if I and other people keep finding you quite *un*acceptable.' That's RET!

W.D. Let's take a project you were involved with – the Gloria film. Now in the Gloria film, at one point Gloria mentions to Rogers that she is contrasting him with her own father and that it would have been nice to have had somebody like Rogers for a father, and Rogers says, 'You seem like a pretty good daughter to me.'

A.E. Yes, that was the later Rogers.

W.D. Would you be critical of that?

A.E. Yes. Suppose I'm Gloria and I'm saying to myself, 'I'm divorced, I'm a pretty shitty person, and I'm not sure about how to raise my daughter. I'm sure I'll never find a good man to love me.' Then I talk to Rogers and he tells me, 'You seem like a pretty good daughter to me.' So I *now* say to myself, 'This therapist, Carl Rogers, who's a nice guy and a famous psychotherapist, says that I seem like a pretty good daughter. Well, if Rogers sees me as a pretty good daughter, I'm obviously a good person!' You see, most of the time that's what clients like Gloria would conclude – 'Because Rogers likes me and thinks I'm a pretty good person, therefore I *am*.' Then she goes out into the world and nobody else thinks she's a pretty good person, so back to shithood she goes!

W.D. Or back to Rogers she goes?

A.E. Yes, she could go back to Rogers forever, because other people still don't care for her now – her men friends, her own daughter – but Rogers *loves* her!

W.D. But isn't that important for people who in their experience of the outside world are surrounded by people who are critical and who really give them a hard time – that they should have at least a minimum of people on their side?

A.E. It's important because they now get contradictory information and they can say, 'Well, not everybody hates me. This therapist loves me, therefore maybe I'm lovable, maybe I can love myself.' But it's still much too conditional; and if they like themselves because their therapist likes them, won't they be anxious about his or her later *not* liking them? And of *any other* significant person not liking them?

W.D. What are some of the other disadvantages of person-created therapy?

A.E. The other disadvantage is that it really isn't direct and honest. For example, Rogers could probably never say to Gloria, 'You know, I think you'd make a pretty good daughter and I can accept you as such. But let's face it, with your daughter and some of the men you want to like you, you are doing some pretty rotten things. You had better stop that crap! I can tell you they dislike you – because you are doing some dislikable things and you had better stop doing those things, even if you are not worthless if you keep doing them.'

So Rogerian therapists may easily be shilly-shallying and dishonest, refusing to face, and to help their clients face, some grim realities. Rogers may say, 'You seem like a pretty good daughter to me', but he may actually be lying! How the hell does he know! So Rogerians often are not direct, not too honest. Also, they don't give homework assignments, they don't give skills training, they don't show people clearly what they believe and feel, and they ignore practically all the effective techniques not only of RET but of other kinds of therapy.

W.D. Most of the person-centred therapists I know will get rather annoyed when they read you saying that, because they argue that they are not aiming to have 'techniques', in the sense that their main purpose is to create the right type of therapeutic climate so that the client can grow and improve.

A.E. But that's another disadvantage – they're romanticists. Carl Rogers, like Rousseau, believed that you are born good and that society makes you bad. So if a therapist accepts you, you can go back to your basic goodness. But RET believes that you are born both good *and* bad – you are born with a propensity of self-hating and self-downing as well as being born with self-actualizing tendencies. This RET view of humans seems to accord with reality, while the person-centred view does not.

W.D. Let's look at another popular humanistically oriented therapy, that is Gestalt therapy. What are your views on the advantages and disadvantages of this therapy?

A.E. Well, the disadvantages are that Gestalt therapy basically has a mystical background, a mystical philosophy which is somewhat close to the Zen Buddhists in that it emphasizes Satori, which means getting in touch with the moment – really smelling the flower or looking at the tea leaves intensely. Then the other aspect of Zen Buddhism is detachment – you don't allow yourself to get too attached to anything. Now the Satori philosophy is good cognitive distraction – when you get in touch with the flower, or the moment, or what's going on in therapy, this will distract you from other things and keep you from worrying about the future. It's an advantage if you stay with the moment and don't go back to the past in Gestalt therapy. But you are not going to get along well in life because you are also blotting out the future. It would also be good to be concerned about saving money, about going to school, about raising your children and so on. So Gestalt therapy ignores problem-solving, skill-training and other practical aspects of therapy that RET and other behavioural therapies include.

The other aspect of it is expressed by Perls' 'famous Gestalt prayer that if we get together that's nice, but if we stay apart then that can't be helped; you go your way and I will go mine. That's close to detachment, that you are involved with yourself and not dependent on others. But then you may not be enough involved with your social group, with politics, with protecting the ecology, with helping your community, and other social concerns. Gestalt therapy is really a feeling therapy; it gets you in touch with your feelings, and that's not bad. But it often encourages you to revel in your feelings and doesn't show you how to change them when they are dysfunctional.

It is also anti-philosophic. I had several debates with Perls on psychological symposia. He would say, 'I'm so *bored* with this rational thinking. It's too intellectual and misses all feeling!' I would then show the audience how unthinking and anti-scientific Fritz was, so that many of his strong followers agreed that I made him look foolish. Gestalt therapy falls short because it *is* anti-intellectual, anti-cognitive, and it doesn't accept that emotional disturbance is largely based on self-sabotaging philosophies and that you had better change your philosophy and act against it if you want to feel better *and* get better.

I particularly find that Gestalt therapy actually encourages people to be angri*er* than before they came to therapy. I often mention the 15-year-old client of mine who was a member of a Gestalt therapy group and also had individual therapy with me, which is unusual. He was in therapy because of his hostility to his parents and to other teenagers. After I had seen him for several sessions, he remarked, 'Every time I go to my Gestalt group, I become angrier, and every time I visit you I become less angry!' You see, Gestalt therapists often encourage hostility!

Now I'll tell you my famous story about Gestalt therapy. A young woman of 28 came to see me because her friend was a member of one of my therapy groups and talked her into joining another of my regular groups after she had a rough experience in a Gestalt therapy group. For a whole year, while she was in it, the leader (a well-known Gestaltist in New York) kept encouraging all the members in the group to express their feelings, especially their feelings of hostility. My client was a slight woman: five feet two inches. One day, a big guy – six feet three inches – who never did like her in the group and often showed this, really got angry at her, slapped her in the face, and pulled her brand-new cashmere sweater at her neck and ripped it completely off, so that she was naked to the waist. Then he slapped her a couple of times more and let her go. The Gestalt group kept cheering him – 'Boy, are you good! Did you really express your feelings! Isn't that great!'

The woman was stunned, and cried for several minutes, ignored by the other seven group members, including three other women. She finally put on her coat and went home in shock and was going to quit the group. But then she said to herself, 'Maybe I saw the situation incorrectly. Maybe he was right to express himself that way. Maybe I unduly provoked him. I'll give it another try.' So she went back to the next group session and to her horror saw that all the other members were again cheering the fellow who assaulted her. 'You know, that was great what you did! You were really in touch with your feelings! You beautifully showed your anger!' She was so horrified that she quit the Gestalt group and couldn't bring herself to go to any therapy for six months. Then her woman friend urged her to come to one of my RET groups. I saw her first for one individual session and said, 'Look, I wouldn't allow anything like what happened to you. If anyone hits anybody in my groups, I immediately stop it, and I say to him right away, if he's angry, "What are you doing to make yourself so angry? You may not like what this other person has done, but what are you irrationally telling yourself to incense yourself about her?"'

W.D. But do you think that incidents like that are inherent in Gestalt therapy, or was it just bad practice, which you can get in any therapy, even RET?

A.E. Many people I've talked to, some of whom were not my clients but people who are Gestalt therapists themselves or in Gestalt therapy, have insisted to me (just like the people in Harvey Jackins's 're-evaluation co-counselling groups do), 'It's very good to express your anger – because underneath your anger you are really depressed.' They subscribe to the psychoanalytic theory that anger covers up depression. So if you get your anger out of your system, you will dissipate it and also become undepressed. It seems that with many feeling therapies, like Gestalt therapy, most of which took their ideas from Wilhelm Reich, go the theory that it's good to express anger.

W.D. But the Gestalt therapists I know in England certainly wouldn't sanction that kind of direct violence.

A.E. No, not every Gestalt group would sanction it and there may be something wrong with that particular therapist, so that's just an extreme case. With my 15-year-old client, nothing like that happened in his group but they definitely trained the group members to be angrier and angrier. However, Erving and Miriam Polster, who do Gestalt therapy in San Diego, seem to be OK and saner than most Gestalt therapists.

W.D. Do you see Gestalt therapy as having any therapeutic advantages?

A.E. The advantage is that you can get in touch with your feelings, and also Gestalt therapists are unwittingly getting clients to do a lot of shame-attacking exercises, without realizing that they *are* shame-attacking. They get you to be honest and open and express your feelings and to acknowledge what's underneath your surface motives; and in the empty chair exercise to enact certain feelings you might not otherwise reveal. So there are some good aspects to Gestalt therapy, if only it included a rational philosophy. In RET we use some of their techniques, for example, the empty chair technique and the hot seat technique in our marathons. But incidentally, these techniques were largely devised by J. L. Moreno, and then Perls took them over and never gave much credit to Moreno.

W.D. Now let's move on to the transpersonal tradition in psychotherapy. I know you have written a recent book about that which has led to controversy (Ellis and Yeager 1989), but what are some of your current views on transpersonal approaches to psychotherapy?

A.E. Well, as you said, I have written a book on it and I will just briefly say why I think transpersonal therapy, or New Age therapy, is a poor kind of therapy. First of all, it is anti-scientific. It sets up hypotheses which are quite unfalsifiable – like Absolute Truth, being at One with the universe, and Unity. Many transpersonalists (or transcendentalists) believe that a table or chair feels as much as humans do. Many of their 'truths' are dogmatic, inflexible, unrealistic and illogical. Transpersonal psychotherapy considerably overlaps with devout religion. Some of its anti-scientific aspects are that it dogmatically upholds such things as extrasensory perception (ESP), pre-cognition, psychokinesis, clairvoyance, ghosts, psychic surgery, fortune-telling, exorcism, monsters, out-of-body phenomena – for all of which we have zero evidence, and almost all of which are produced by charlatans, as Randi the Magician and others have shown. But transpersonal therapists say that psychic phenomena indubitably exist and by tapping into them you get miraculous results. Transpersonal therapy will not abide uncertainty nor accept probability. It demands *absolute* knowledge and has a need for certainty, for dogma, and tries to achieve certainty through astrology, fortune-telling, tarot cards and other magical means. It refuses to accept the inevitable grim aspects of life and Pollyanna-ishly makes claims for total internal peace and ineffable bliss. At the same time, it is often fatalistic, and passively tolerates many undesirable things that *could* be changed, because that is supposedly our karma. Again, it espouses all kinds of magic and miracle 'solutions' to pain and disturbance, such as reincarnation and afterlife. It's anti-humanistic in many respects because while we in RET go for human life and survival, transpersonalists go for superhuman goals and for the idea that humans should submit to some kind of supreme guru or deity. New Age therapy is often dictatorial, fascistic, cultish and in danger of ending up with terrorism, such as that espoused by Jim Jones and the Ayatollah Khomeini.

W.D. I just wanted to raise that – it almost appears in your book as if you include the Ayatollah as a transpersonal psychologist!

A.E. Yes, because he was devout, and devoutness is where transpersonalists, rigid religionists and terrorists overlap – they often firmly believe in Absolute Truth. They think they are 100 per cent right and that the rest of us are 100 per cent wrong – and that if we don't abide by their Absolute Truth, we may well deserve to die.

W.D. What you are saying is that if taken to extremes, transpersonal psychology will lead you to the Ayatollah? But the Ayatollah wasn't a transpersonal psychologist!

A.E. No, he was not a psychologist, but he believed in transcendentalism, reincarnation, and transpersonalism. I debated this at the American Psychological Association's group interested in transpersonal psychology and they tried to tell me that their brand of transpersonal psychology wasn't transcendentalist at all and that they just believe in certain unusual aspects of psychology. But I contend that transpersonal psychologists and therapists are transcendentalists at bottom philosophically, that they are really devout and religious. They may *say* they don't believe in all the New Age cults, but as far as I can see they really encourage them.

Transpersonal therapy also blocks profound philosophic change; it doesn't go after irrational musts, dogmas and rigidities and try to get people to surrender them. It blocks insight and awareness by appealing to a 'higher consciousness' and to supernatural 'insights' which are unfalsifiable. It's against unconditional self-acceptance because it advocates conditional self-acceptance. When you accept Absolute Truth, sacredness, or the guru or god of a particular cult, then and only then are you OK. But if you don't accept this guru or New Age sect, they may literally kill you, as happened with Jim Jones's followers in Guyana.

W.D. But again, isn't that outside the range of convenience of transpersonal psychotherapists? Aren't you in danger of taking somebody like Jim Jones, who as far as I know wasn't a licensed therapist, and tarnishing the whole field of transpersonal psychology with that brush?

A.E. Well, that's true to some degree, so I'd better not overgeneralize. But I still contend that most transpersonalists and New Age therapists uphold a transcendental, mystical philosophy that can easily lead to cultism, dogma and even terrorism. While if we stay with science and abjure mysticism, we will almost never promote occult and potentially harmful therapeutic cults.

W.D. Do you see transpersonal therapy as having any advantages?

A.E. The big advantage is that most of the transpersonal groups, I won't say all of them, in some sense believe that you can create your own emotional destiny and that you can change it. So they believe in one of the basic precepts of RET and cognitive-behaviour therapy – that you make yourself disturbed and that by believing in our group, our cult, our ritual you can undisturb yourself. Also, many of them are very nice people who are against dictatorship, war and atomic weapons, though many others are extremists like the Ayatollah Khomeini and Jim Jones.

W.D. Now let's move on to the next major tradition, which includes RET, and that is the cognitive-behavioural tradition which you obviously favour and believe has distinct advantages. Perhaps, however, for the purpose of this interview, we could look at some of the *dis*advantages that the cognitive-behavioural therapeutic tradition has.

A.E. Well, cognitive-behaviour therapy includes a wide variety of effective techniques but it has been accused, for example by Mike Mahoney and Vittorio Guidano, of being too mechanistic and rationalistic, of favouring associationism, and of missing the underlying and tacit philosophic assumptions behind people's disturbances. They may be right about some of the cognitive-behavioural therapies, especially the problem-solving ones and the skill-training ones, because considerable cognitive-behaviour therapy consists of problem-solving, skill-training, relaxation techniques, biofeedback, stress reduction and other methods that tend to be mechanistic and non-philosophic. But RET, even more than Mahoney and Guidano, examines and Disputes clients' deep-structured, tacit philosophies, that people *construct* and *invent* rather than acquire from association-acquired experiences or teachings. Mahoney and Guidano, in their form of cognitive-behaviour therapy, insist on a pretty profound constructivism, as RET has done for many years. Like Richard Wessler, they somewhat contradict their own constructivism by agreeing with the psychoanalysts and overemphasizing early childhood influences on emotional disturbance. Guidano particularly goes back to early childhood, while RET says that even in early childhood we *construct* our *musts* and *demands* about our experiences and we continue to actively *recreate* our self-defeating demands as we grow older. Therefore, we had better understand our present constructions, which we are still actively evolving and can therefore change, rather than dwelling too much on our past constructions, which are interesting but which may have been quite different from our present philosophies, and which in any event we can't erase.

The cognitive-behaviour therapies are also accused of being superficial and I agree that many of them are, because they miss the deep philosophic underpinnings of disturbance and often only Dispute clients' unrealistic attributions and inferences, while ignoring the rigid, imperative musts that lie behind them. They are also accused of staying too much in the present and ignoring the past, but I say that's usually legitimate. In RET, we can show people how in the past they thought crookedly, but endlessly going over the pattern of the past is largely a waste of time because by *understanding* past patterns (if one really *does* see them accurately instead of inventing what they *supposedly* were), one may *feel* good unearthing one's history, but I found no evidence, when I practised psychoanalysis, that this kind of historical insight helped my clients to *change* their dysfunctional philosophies and thereby *get* better. Digging intensively into a client's past, as some cognitive-behavioural constructivists advocate, may unearth some fascinating material, but I have usually found it to be wasteful and side-tracking. 'Deep' therapy of this nature is not necessarily efficient!

W.D. What do you think as the disadvantages of the constructivistic approach of Mahoney and Guidano?

A.E. Well, Mahoney and Guidano include several things in their constructivism that are of dubious value – such as, as I just pointed out, they go *ad nauseam* into the past. They're really reviving psychoanalysis!

W.D. It seems to me that Mahoney is now arguing that quite a bit of what we call client resistance is, if you like, natural and needs to be respected and that meaningful deep personality change takes a long time, and he advocates long-term therapy and is quite critical of brief therapy as far as I understand it.

A.E. Yes, and I think he's right, if he would only make clear that he is talking about borderline clients. He implies that practically no neurotics can have effective brief therapy. I think he really means that therapists are not properly diagnosing their borderline clients, who might improve a little with brief therapy but who have such rotten underlying philosophies and who hold on to them so rigidly that they often resist regular treatment and often require long-term treatment. Also, as I note in my book, *Overcoming Resistance* (Ellis 1985), resistant clients often require quite forceful RET and not the kind of gentle cognitive-behaviour therapy that Mahoney and Guidano seem to do.

W.D. What do you think is the main advantage of RET over other approaches within the cognitive-behavioural tradition?

A.E. First of all, RET assumes that people create or construct their underlying dysfunctional philosophies, while most other cognitive-behaviour therapies assume that they learn it from their parents and culture. We assume that they originally constructed –

and are still actively constructing – these demanding philosophies. So we more actively and forcefully try to help them to change their constructions.

Second, RET assumes that people also have innate self-actualizing tendencies. So we not only work hard to help them make anti-disturbance changes, but also to actualize and fulfil themselves more – to achieve maximum enjoyment.

Third, we are almost the only cognitive-behavioural therapy truly offering unconditional acceptance, and teaching people how to achieve it without resorting to any religious or mystical trappings. I think RET is the only cognitive-behavioural therapy that really forcefully teaches clients how to be anti-musturbatory, anti-dogmatic and pro-scientific. We teach people how to be good open-minded scientists while the other therapies sort of skirt over that, though they may implicitly accept it.

W.D. In Beck's approach the relationship between therapist and client is said to be one of collaborative empiricism, so perhaps he focuses on the empirical aspect of science.

A.E. Well, first of all, that's an exaggerated claim. If Tim Beck really stuck rigidly to collaboratism, that would be a therapeutic disadvantage. Because almost any good cognitive-behavioural therapist knows more, much more, than the client and does more direct teaching than 'collaboration'. Beck implies that he and his followers are *equal* collaborators with their clients – which I very much doubt! They are probably trying to show how 'nice' they are as therapists compared to us more direct RET 'ruffians!' They refuse honestly to acknowledge that virtually *all* effective therapists – including psychoanalytic, person-centred and Gestalt therapists – know much more about therapeutic change than their clients do, and had better not be therapists *unless* they do! Because therapists are more knowledgeable and specifically trained than are the clients, they (subtly or honestly) *direct* their sessions with these clients – no matter how 'non-directive' or 'collaborative' they pretend to be.

W.D. Now, two approaches to therapy that are currently in vogue are NLP (Neurolinguistic Programming) and Ericksonian approaches to therapy. What are your views on these two approaches?

A.E. I read the NLP book, *The Structure of Magic* (Bandler and Grinder 1975), and found that they have some interesting techniques that they largely took from other schools. But their basic theory assumes that when you say the same thing in different sensory ways, it means quite different things to the listener. If a client is naturally (biologically) a hearing-centred, rather than a seeing-centred person, you therefore have to say, 'I hear you', rather than 'I see what you mean', in order to reach him and get him to buy your message. If you use the wrong sensory modality with him or her, your therapy will presumably be completely ineffective. Moreover, if you are a salesperson and you learn through NLP exactly what sensory modality your customers favour, you can use this modality and easily sell them the Brooklyn Bridge!

Thus NLP theory not only has very little evidence behind it, but Allport and Vernon in the 1930s did a series of studies showing that the correlation between the way you sense things and the way you act on them or think about them is very low, about 0.2 or 0.3, and I don't see any evidence in therapy either that NLP theory works. Many of their communications techniques are based on this dubious theory.

NLP workshops train people in NLP and give them certificates even if they have no education whatsoever, provided they take enough courses. That's why they are so popular. No matter who you are, you can get an NLP certificate and then do therapy yourself.

I think NLP has a few sound techniques, including reframing, a cognitive method it has taken over from Paul Watzlawick and from RET; and those techniques are sometimes effective. But they also claim that in ten minutes they can cure anyone of a lifetime phobia. That's a bit much!

About nine studies have been done using NLP with control groups and they all show that its main sensory modality technique is ineffective. But, like several other therapies, NLPers mainly seem to use poor techniques which don't work, then throw in a few good ones which are effective, and then claim that the poor techniques do work.

We have the same danger in RET, because we use a variety of techniques and we could say that it's RET Disputing that actually works, when maybe it's our *in vivo* desensitization or our shame-attacking exercises that do the trick. But at least RET techniques are derived in conjunction with our cognitive-emotive-behavioural theory of disturbance and of personality change. Thus, we use *in vivo* desensitization because our theory holds that when you act against an irrational belief you tend to change it. Many therapies, like NLP, are more eclectic than integrative, do things more or less at random and use any technique that works. That's OK if they honestly espouse eclecticism. But it is not OK if they use numerous methods that have nothing to do with their theory and then maintain that the one really derived from this theory really did the trick. So I am highly sceptical that NLP technique really works for the theoretical reasons given by Bandler and Grinder.

W.D. Now what about Ericksonian approaches?

A.E. Well, Milton Erickson claimed that indirect techniques are more powerful than directly telling people what to do, though actually Jay Haley (1973) has said in his book on Erickson that Erickson himself mostly used direct suggestion as well as some indirect techniques. But the Ericksonians today, maybe to be different, insist that it is Erickson's indirect techniques that work. Now the trouble with the indirect approach is first of all that it has an element of dishonesty. Erickson made up all kinds of stories and then claimed, without confirming evidence, that they produced miraculous cures.

W.D. How can you be so sure of that?

A.E. Oh, you can divine it from reading his books; and several very reputable hypnotic therapists – such as Ernest Hilgard – have pointed out that he was a great story-teller and that he made up all kinds of things that he didn't necessarily believe in, though he obviously designed them so that the person who was listening would believe him. His approach also lacks steady self-repetition of rational self-statements. According to the Ericksonian hypothesis, you do a new behaviour that Erickson tells you to try, and you only do it once and it changes you for the rest of your life. Now that's very unlikely! In RET we hold that you teach clients something several times and then they have to repeat it many times – that's what really works. With Erickson, the client doesn't have to work and practise. Although he did give homework assignments, he assumed that you just had to change your outlook and your actions once and then you magically changed. For instance you do something paradoxical and presumably for the rest of your life you're different. Well, that's improbable!

So the Ericksonian approach de-emphasizes the philosophy of hard work. It looks easy and that's why clients may take to it. That's also why therapists take to it because they think, 'Oh, we now have a magic formula for speaking directly to your unconscious. You really don't want to change but we'll quickly trick you into doing so in spite of your unconscious resistance'. Ericksonian methods reinforce clients' gullibility. You do what the *therapist* wants you to do instead of, as in RET, learning how to scientifically think for yourself. It reinforces devoutness – you become devoutly attached to the therapist and you take him or her as a guru. It has a strong element of conformity in it.

Practically no outcome studies of Ericksonian therapy have been done. It may well work with a small minority of clients, but it's made to look like it works with all of them. Erickson probably tried the same technique a hundred times and it worked once or twice. Then he implied, 'This will always work!' The Freudians do the same thing.

Ericksonian methods assume unconscious resistance – they are based on the idea that people unconsciously resist change so let's slither into their unconscious and get rid of the resistance. Actually much of what we call resistance is quite conscious. It may have unconscious motivations – the belief, 'It *shouldn't* be so hard for me to change! It's too hard!' – but people often know they resist and they know they don't do their homework, so their resistance is not deeply unconscious. Ericksonian therapy ignores resistance stemming from low frustration tolerance (LFT) and ignores the LFT *philosophy* behind much resistance. So it doesn't try to help clients change this life-is-too-hard and therapy-shouldn't-be-so-hard philosophy. It only has anecdotal evidence for it, virtually no controlled studies have ever been done for Ericksonian therapy. Ericksonians claim that direct methods won't work; therefore, therapists must concentrate on indirect methods where their unconscious presumably speaks to their clients' unconscious. This is a very implausible hypothesis – and ignores the fact that millions of people improve by reading books, by listening to cassettes, by going to talks, by hearing sermons, and through other forms of didactic therapy. In other words, they change themselves through very direct methods of therapy. Ericksonianism assumes that disturbed people who are directly helped hardly exist; but of course millions of them do.

W.D. Now what do you think are the main advantages of this approach to therapy?

A.E. It is very persuasive. It prescribes homework and induces clients to assume, through suggestion, that this homework will work. So it sometimes persuades them – more directly than indirectly – to think and act differently. And it uses analogies and stories, it's emotive and evocative in many ways, and it uses reframing. It is anti-psychoanalytic, it doesn't go into the past, and it does indicate that people have innate irrationalities, though I don't think it shows them how to get rid of them. It uses manipulation and influence, which sometimes work, and it encourages strategic planning by the therapist.

The one outstanding thing that Erickson pointed out is that in using hypnosis you don't have to put the client very directly or deeply into a trance. You don't have to say, 'Relax, relax, you are going into a deep hypnotic state'. You can hypnotize people by indirect suggestion; and many people go into a light trance when they listen to indirect suggestion. Ericksonian hypnosis is not the old kind of hypnosis, but a light tricky kind that can be useful with some people who won't *listen* or follow other kinds of suggestion. If you have tried direct RET or other methods and none of them works, if your clients simply won't do their homework, then you might as well try some Ericksonian semi-magical, supposedly unconscious techniques. However, I would say, use them as a last resort, and don't exaggerate their effectiveness – as the Ericksonians often do!

W.D. Now the other major trend across the whole field of psychotherapy is the movement towards eclecticism and integration. What are your views on the strengths and weaknesses of that particular trend?

A.E. I think that RET was the first among the modern therapies to pioneer the idea of being integrative, though we didn't originally use that term. To be integrative means that you have a basic theory of what works in therapy and then you use a variety of techniques that fit into your theory. You don't use them eclectically – that is, you don't use any techniques under the sun just because they happen at times to work. But you stick largely with a good many cognitive, emotive and behavioural methods that are consonant with your theory and that partially seem to confirm it. That's what RET has always done.

People think that because RET emphasizes direct (as well as less direct) and vigorous (as well as more easy-going) Disputing that we *only* argue people out of their irrational Beliefs. Wrong! RET includes a large number of cognitive techniques, many emotive-evocative techniques (not just rational-emotive imagery and shame-attacking), and a good many behavioural techniques. But all of these we normally use fit right into the RET theory. We don't use *any* technique *at random*, to see if it works, but use those that we think there *is* reason to believe, according to our *theory*, will work quickest and best. I doubt whether any psychotherapy is randomly eclectic. I think all therapists choose techniques in relation to who the client is and also in relation to their theory, even when they don't enunciate the theory very clearly.

Arnold Lazarus, who is often thought of as being quite eclectic, actually follows social learning theory, which he may not enunciate clearly, but which he does follow. Psychoanalysts are obviously following a theory; so are the Gestalt and existentialist therapists. I don't know of anyone who is truly just eclectic. Therapists sometimes say they are, but I think they always have a basic theory and then they fit their 'eclectic' techniques into it. RET has always integrated many techniques with its basic theory. We have our *usual* practices; but we are, because of our theoretical opposition to dogma and rigidity, so flexible in our practice that at times we can even use techniques that are *against* our theory when the ones *for* our theory don't work. Thus RET theory opposes devout, absolutist religiosity. But if regular RET isn't working with a client and this client doesn't allow any rational methods to work, a RETer may use this client's disturbance – that is her or his devoutness – to help her or him improve. We can use almost anything that works, but *normally* employ regular RET methods and only *occasionally* use *irrational* techniques.

It is interesting that about ten years ago Marvin Goldfried (1980) wrote his well-known paper on the advantages of eclecticism and integration but ignored several of their disadvantages. If we are *too* integrative, we imply that some *poor* techniques (like classical psychoanalytic techniques) are desirable when many of them hardly work at all or are often iatrogenic. Marvin and some other integrationists want to be open and include all major therapies in their integrationist attempts. But they fail to point out that some techniques will *sometimes* work, but they *mostly* won't, or that they are *sometimes* beneficial, but *mostly* harmful. Therapists, I contend, function better when they have a theory, because a theory can more or less be tested (although it's difficult to do so), and it can be seen whether therapists' main view of disturbance and therapy, and the techniques they use are efficient and effective. Many young therapists are endorsing eclecticism but I don't think they are asking themselves two important questions. (1) 'Do the techniques we use fit in with our theory?', and (2) 'Are they efficient for this particular client?' Those are the two questions I would like eclectic and integrative psychotherapists to ask themselves.

W.D. So it seems to me that the dangers you see in eclecticism are first, the lack of good theoretical underpinnings to encourage therapists to choose techniques appropriately, and second, that in a desire to be open to all kinds of techniques, therapists choose and use 'poor' techniques in the spirit of openness.

A.E. That's right, and the latest example is Guidano and Mahoney, who are now emphasizing some psychoanalytic methods, such as exploring the client's early childhood at great length. If they really do this, they can easily lead many clients up the garden path for a year or two or three and belatedly get around to the more effective cognitive-behavioural techniques. If so, I think they will then do much more harm than good.

W.D. What do you make of the research that quite a few people quote, that apart from certain specific conditions there seems to be an equivalence of effectiveness across specific approaches to psychotherapy?

A.E. I am quite sceptical about that conclusion because I think that practically almost all studies of psychotherapy, with few exceptions, have measured whether people *feel* better and not whether they *get* better. In terms of feeling better, some of the worst techniques will get pretty good results. In psychoanalysis, if we take only the people who stay and forget those who leave – because it has been shown that most clients leave psychoanalysis pretty quickly – we find that they stay partly because they do feel better and they like what's going on. Maybe they like the fact that they can indulge in endless whining, can blame their parents for all their disturbances, and can continue in therapy without pushing their asses to change themselves.

In person-centred therapy, clients certainly enjoy the therapist telling them, 'I really like you, you're OK', and things like that, and at the end of ten or twenty sessions they are definitely going to feel better! Now some of them will conclude, 'I can now see that I am not a shit after all', and conclude it for the right reasons. But most of them will probably conclude, 'I am not a shit *because* my therapist likes me and *because* we have a good relationship'. According to RET, this is the *wrong* reason for self-acceptance. So I think that practically all the research into therapy is still oriented towards how much better you *feel*, and there are practically no accurate criteria for how much better you *are*.

W.D. Let me play devil's advocate for a minute. The criticism I have heard of you is that when research doesn't go in accord with your own notions, then you question the methodology of the research. Like in this case you say that most outcome studies measure how people feel better rather than get better, but if the research has shown that RET was superior to other approaches, you wouldn't make such criticisms!

A.E. That's true, everybody tends to do that. We like the research that bolsters our own theory and practice and we find reasons why the research that doesn't is not good research. So that's a common bias of any theoretician or any practitioner of therapy. And because we all tend to (irrationally) do that, it would be nice if we had some really objective outcome studies. Don't forget that most studies which show the effectiveness of RET and other kinds of therapy are done by people who favour the brand they are testing. What objectivity! All research is to be viewed sceptically because of the biases of the researchers. It's hard to eliminate such bias, and the only way I can think of is to keep refining the research instruments and the criteria, and to have favouring and disfavouring researchers continually keep trying to falsify new and old theories and practices.

Although I am naturally biased in favour of RET studies, I did point out in the book, *Inside Rational-Emotive Therapy* (Bernard and DiGiuseppe 1989), that although outcome studies for RET are usually favourable, they do not as yet show as good results as the outcome studies for Beck's cognitive therapy. Fortunately, from my prejudiced view, Beck's therapy overlaps a great deal with RET, so that practically all the cognitive therapy studies implicitly support RET. More importantly, of the scores of outcomes studies that have supported RET, exceptionally few studies have been done using RET as a whole. Instead, the existing studies tend to focus on one aspect of RET, especially cognitive restructuring, which is only one *part* of what is almost always done in rational-emotive therapy. So to empirically support the effectiveness of RET, a whole new set of studies had better be done and they had better use a definitive RET manual.

W.D. And also even if studies had been done using the full range of RET techniques you still have the problem of answering the question, 'Did the RET practised in these studies meet the criterion of good RET?'

A.E. That's right. Another factor that confuses outcome research is that RET is hardly separate from behaviour therapy, but *includes* many common behavioural methods. So when RET works, it is often not clear whether it is the behavioural and/or its cognitive methods that are more effective. These questions are difficult to research, but eventually can be investigated with controlled studies. The vast majority of studies of RET are minor studies, with twelve or so people in them, often over a period of about ten weeks, and they often don't follow up a year or two later. Incidentally a few studies do seem to show that even when RET is no more effective in the short term than some other techniques, like interpersonal therapy, when followed up a year or two later the RET improvements are better maintained. So RET ultimately brings about better results.

But research studies are definitely in their formative stages as yet and we can't prove too much by them; we just get indications that RET is effective. There are now about five hundred studies that tend to show that RET and other forms of cognitive-behaviour therapy (CBT) get better results than a control group – a waiting-list group, a pure behaviour therapy group, or an interpersonal therapy group. So we can say there is some evidence that RET and CBT work, though no conclusive evidence that they are more effective than other modes of treatment.

W.D. And again, as we said earlier, it doesn't prove that if RET *does* work that it works for the reasons we say that it does!

A.E. That's right.

5 PERSONAL ISSUES

WINDY DRYDEN In this last interview I want to look at the interface between the personal and professional aspects of yourself. Now as you look back over the years, can you think of any experiences that may have encouraged you to enter into the profession of psychotherapy?

ALBERT ELLIS Yes, there were some such experiences. I was first going to be a writer of fiction, poetry and plays and then I decided that I wasn't going to be able to support myself in that manner. I was not the Great American Novelist that I wanted to be – so I started to write non-fiction. I wrote books on economics, leadership and organization because I was interested in the radical movement. In my early twenties I actually translated Karl Marx from abstruse into simple English. I took the whole three volumes of *Das Kapital* and put it into simple question-and-answer form and it got tentatively accepted by Oxford University Press, who said it was better than John Strachey's book, *The Nature of Capitalism*. Strachey simplified Volume One, but I rewrote all three volumes, because I wanted the revolutionary movement to understand Karl Marx so that they *wouldn't* swear by him! I thought that his theory of surplus value was unrealistic and unfalsifiable – and many years later I was delighted to find that Karl Popper came to the same conclusion. I could have got my simplification of Marx published if I would allow either the American Communist or Socialist party to endorse it. But although I was quite radical, I strongly opposed the Communist party for being dictatorial and a handmaiden of the Soviet Union Communists and also opposed the Socialist party for being too wishy-washy. I later gave up being a communist with a small c, because I saw that communism was essentially dictatorial and anti-democratic and that although capitalism has its serious flaws, it tends to espouse freedom and be more efficient than Soviet-type communism. So I gave up trying to get my book on Marxism published and decided to write books on sex, love and marriage, especially one entitled *The Case for Promiscuity*, which was apparently too liberal to get published when I wrote it in the 1930s.

In order to complete the 2,000-page manuscript I wrote on this work, I read hundreds of books and articles on sex, love and marriage, and when my friends realized I was writing a book on sex, they came to me with their sex, love and marriage problems, and to my surprise I found that I was fairly good at helping them solve their problems. So I opened the LAMP Institute (LAMP stood for Love and Marriage Problems) on my own. Then I was told by my lawyer that I had better go and get official status because he thought the Catholics would get me because I was sexually very liberal. So then I decided to go for my PhD degree because I liked doing sex and relationship counselling for my friends and relatives – I wasn't doing it for paying clients yet – and I enjoyed doing research in the field and thought it would be a good profession. At that time, there were no degrees in sex therapy or even marital and family therapy, so I decided to go for one in clinical psychology.

W.D. How suitable did you think you would be for a career in psychotherapy?

A.E. I thought I was very suitable for a psychotherapeutic career because I was a pioneer of sex therapy – there were very few sex therapists then – and I was one of the first psychologists to become a sex therapist. I liked sex and marital therapy because of the teaching aspect. Like the early sexologists – Havelock Ellis, Iwan Bloch, August Forel, Magnus Hirschfeld and others – all of whom where physicians, I directly asked people about their sex-love problems, taught them what to do differently, gave them homework, and later checked to see how they carried it out. Also, because I had written another unpublished manuscript, 'The art of never making yourself desperately unhappy', I was interested in showing my clients how to refuse to make themselves miserable and to lead happier lives. I also enjoyed the propaganda aspect of the work I began to do in sex, love and marriage, because I stoutly favoured sexual freedom. I was a sexual libertarian and I wanted to get rid of sex censorship and let people do what they wanted to do with their love lives. I was still trying to get *The Case for Sexual Promiscuity* published, but all the publishers in the 1930s and 1940s found it too *risqué*. I later published Volume One, *The Case for Sexual*

Liberty, (Ellis 1965) in 1965, after I had already become a well-known psychologist and author and when sexual liberalism had become much more fashionable. After I received my MA degree in clinical psychology in 1943, and the licensing of psychologists in New York State was still a decade away, I established a part-time practice as a psychotherapist, sex therapist and marriage and family therapist and became a pioneering psychologist in the last two fields. I thoroughly enjoyed showing people how to have better sex and love relationships and like being simultaneously involved in sexual politics as well as helping people clinically.

W.D. Now in terms of becoming an analyst, you almost went from the sublime to the ridiculous in terms of activity levels. Did becoming an analyst go against your natural tendency to be active and efficient?

A.E. Yes, it did, and yet in some ways it didn't. At first, I did orthodox analysis with people on the sofa and I just sat behind them and recorded a lot of material and listened and listened. I did it in a fairly orthodox fashion because my analyst, who was a follower of Karen Horney, did it in that fashion. He had been a Freudian analyst for twenty-five years in Berlin and then he became a follower of Horney and an existentialist, so his interpretations were different, but he practised classical analysis, where analysands lie on a sofa, free associate, and do dream analysis and so on. So I did all of that but I quickly discovered that I couldn't do it four of five times a week (and even my analyst did it only twice a week) because people couldn't afford to pay for it. So then I started gravitating soon to psychoanalytically oriented psychotherapy, which is a brief form of psychoanalysis where the client sits up and you both face each other. You go through the client's past fairly briefly and then start actively interpreting it in terms of the present. So that was much more active and directive psychotherapy than was classical analysis. Some psychoanalytically oriented therapists, like Franz Alexander and Thomas French, were really doing a different kind of analysis even back then, and Ferenczi invented a form of therapy called active psychoanalysis. So when I was practising my own brand of psychoanalytic therapy that didn't go against my grain, but when I did classical analysis that was somewhat against my personal inclination to be active and directive.

W.D. Were there no lingering doubts about your own suitability for the field of psychotherapy?

A.E. No, I enjoyed showing people the error of their ways and pointing out how they made themselves miserable and how they could stop doing so. As I noted above, one of my early books, which never got published, was called 'The art of never making yourself desperately unhappy'. I was interested in the psychology of happiness, which I derived from reading ancient philosophies – especially Epictetus, Marcus Aurelius and Confucius – and from modern philosophers – especially Ralph Waldo Emerson, Henry David Thoreau, George Santayana, John Dewey and Bertrand Russell. I read a lot of books on happiness, so I thought that some of it was good stuff, that I could adapt it and that I could teach people how to be happier. So being a psychotherapist was right up my alley and from the start I thoroughly enjoyed it.

W.D. How does working as a therapist fit in with the rest of your life?

A.E. It has become the major aspect of my life and was even informally a part of it before I became a professional therapist. First of all, when I was interested in radical politics, around the age of 21 I read an interesting book, *Psychopathology and Politics*, written in 1933 or so by Harold Lasswell, a professor of political science. He said that people in the radical movement were nutty, that they had psychopathology, and as an active leader in that movement I could see he was right. So I said to my radical friends, 'You know, we are not in the movement just because we read Karl Marx and we think capitalism is wrong and socialism is a better system. We actually have strong ties to radicalism because we have some emotional problems that lead us to intensively rebel.' They wouldn't believe me, thought I was crazy, and were sure they had pure intellectual motives for their radicalism. So I got interested in psychopathology. I had read just about all of Freud in college, because at the age of 16 I entered Baruch School of City College, located right next to the famous Russell Sage Library in New York, which had mainly sociology and psychology books. I borrowed books by the car-load from this library – sometimes ten or more every week. I enjoyed reading Freud, Adler, Jung and other therapists and even got over some of my sexual hang-ups by reading Freud, because in a sense he was very liberal about masturbation, oral relations and other sex practices. But I could see from the start that Freud was a non-scientist and an extremist, so I was never an arch-Freudian. When I later practised psychoanalysis, I followed Erich Fromm, Karen Horney and Harry Stack Sullivan more than the classical Freudians.

Anyway, in my early twenties, when I got myself over my

shyness in approaching women and started regular dating, I knew a lot about psychology and especially about the psychology and philosophy of happiness, because that was my hobby. So whenever I went out with a woman, I found out all about her life and her personal problems and soon discovered that all the women I dated were nutty – especially my first wife, she was very nutty! – and I started to unofficially give them therapy and found that I greatly enjoyed doing so.

To this day, if I go to a cocktail party and meet a new person, man or woman, and they want to talk about their problems, I am always willing to help them. I like doing that because normal conversation often bores me shitless. People say the same thing over and over and, even when they talk about politics or economics, in which I am somewhat interested, they repeat the same things. Or else they talk about the movies or TV shows they saw and stuff like that, and I am just not that interested. I used to be exceptionally involved in political, social and economic problems, but then I got more interested in personal human problems, so you could say that became the main core of my life. That's why I got along so well with women in my twenties and thereafter. I used to say that I probably had the highest percentage of laying women on the first night of any male in New York City in the 1930s and 1940s. Because I talked to the women I dated about their problems for two or three hours. Then they really liked me because they could see that I was interested in them personally and not just in their tits and asses. So they'd go to bed with me in a very high percentage of cases because I was doing what women to this day complain that men don't sufficiently do – talk about their own and the woman's feelings!

W.D. Was that a strategy on your part?

A.E. No, it wasn't a strategy. It *became* partially a strategy when I saw how well it worked. But I really enjoyed it! Because, you see, when I met a new woman I wanted to know all about her life and her problems, partly to see whether she was OK for me – because that's valuable information. But also because I just like that kind of thing. I'd talk about my date's interests in art or science or whatever, but I especially liked to hear about her relations with her family, her previous lovers, her sex life and married life; and we always soon got to her problems. Sex, love and marriage problems – that's always been my special thing! So in my social life in my early years I ferreted out considerably personal information which I later used in my therapy formulations and practices.

W.D. Now you have talked about how people can overcome their problems, particularly their anxieties, by repeatedly exposing themselves to what they are scared of. That parallels how you overcame some of your own problems, doesn't it?

A.E. Exactly. The main things I did were to force myself to speak in public and to talk to women in the Bronx Botanical Gardens, and then there were shame-attacking exercises I invented like the one about the cafeterias.

W.D. Let's go over all three of them, because the readers won't necessarily know about them. Let's go over the public-speaking anxiety first.

A.E. Well, until the age of 19 I was scared shitless of public speaking and never spoke in public if I could help it. On one occasion, I had won a prize in Sunday school and all I had to do was to go up and say 'Thank you' and take the prize, and when I sat down my friend next to me said, 'What are you crying about?' Because my eyes were watering from anxiety. The same thing happened in public school a little later when I had read a paragraph I had selected from a newspaper. When I sat down, my friend next to me said, 'What are you crying for?' I was so anxious about my public presentation, even just reading or saying thank you, that I always avoided it. I got a little better because I had to take four courses in public speaking in college. I hated them and wouldn't have taken a single one if they hadn't forced me to do so.

Then at the age of 19 I joined a radical political group. I was one of the leaders and I was supposed to go and speak in public against war and fascism and for revolutionary democracy. Of course, I didn't want to do it. But then I went back to the books I had been reading on the philosophy of happiness, some of which said that if you force yourself to do what you're your afraid of, you can overcome your irrational fears. I also read John B. Watson's famous experiment where he put a rabbit at one end of the table and a rabbit-phobic kid at the other and gradually moved the rabbit closer to the kid – until the child became desensitized and began to pet the rabbit. *In vivo* desensitization!

So I said to myself, 'Shit, if it's good enough for kiddies, it's good enough for me!' and I made myself speak and speak and speak in public, and after about ten times I not only got over my fear of public speaking, as I had thought I would, but to my surprise I found that I had an innate knack for it, a natural fluency which I had never suspected! A few years later, one of the greatest public speakers I ever met, Abe Stone, who wrote books on sex and who used to be invited to be chairman of meetings mainly because he told jokes so well, came up to me spontaneously and said, 'Ellis, I've never heard anybody as fluent as you.' And I was the one who never spoke in public! So I kept speaking and speaking, and got over my irrational fear. Once I deliberately made myself *un*comfortable, I became comfortable and finally began to enjoy it. Now you can't keep me away from the public-speaking platform! So by *telling myself* cognitively that nothing terrible would happen if I *did* speak poorly and was disapproved of for doing so and by *acting* against my phobia, I made a 180-degree circle and completely overcame it.

I then told myself, 'Hell, what's more important than public speaking?' And the answer was, 'Sex and love'. I was scared about encountering any new women whom I found desirable. At 19 I lusted after 101 out of 100 females but I never approached any of them. I had to be introduced by my friends. I went to the Bronx Botanical Gardens, near my home, about 200 days every year – to read my books and to flirt with females. I sat on a bench about ten feet away from another bench on which an attractive woman was sitting. I looked at the women and they looked back at me and some of them were obviously interested, but I always made up excuses not to speak to them. Some of them were eager and would walk slowly away from where they were sitting, hoping that I would follow them, but I always made up an excuse, such as, 'They're too young – or too old!' 'They're too tall or too dark!' 'They're too blue-eyed or too brown-eyed!' I had a million excuses and never talked to any of them.

I finally told myself, 'Screw this! These excuses will get me nowhere – only help me keep my phobia!' So I convinced myself that nothing catastrophic or terrible would happen if I did approach a number of women and got rejected. And I gave myself a specific homework assignment. I was on vacation in June and I determined to go to the Botanical Gardens every day and whenever I saw a woman sitting on a park bench alone I would sit next to her on the same bench – not a bench ten feet away, where I usually sat – and talk to her within one minute, yes, within one minute after I sat down. Following my homework assignment, I found 130 women sitting alone on park benches that month – all shapes, sizes and ages. No excuses! I sat next to *all* of them. About thirty got up and waltzed away immediately, but that left me an even sample of a hundred – good for research purposes!

I spoke to the whole hundred, no exceptions, no debate – about the birds, the flowers, the trees, their knitting, the book they were reading, anything and everything. Well, if Fred Skinner had been writing at the time – he was probably in graduate school then because he was about ten years older than me – he would have said my approaches to women should have been extinguished. Because out of the hundred women I spoke to, I only made *one* date – and she never showed up! But despite this total lack of reinforcement, I got completely over my fear of approaching strange women. Because I saw *cognitively* that nobody took out a stiletto and cut my balls off, nobody vomited and ran away, nobody called a cop, nobody did anything bad to me while rejecting me. Instead, I had a hundred pleasant conversations! My basic goal – to go to bed with all the women I approached – was completely thwarted. None the less, I got completely over my fear and have been able to talk to women whenever I wanted to for the rest of my life. Also, because I *practised* talking to the hundred women I approached, I got much better at interpersonal conversation and dated several of the next hundred I approached!

Then I invented a real shame-attacking exercise, which even at that time I saw as being shame-attacking, long before I was even thinking of becoming a therapist. I had this group of friends in Poe Park and I used to go there almost every night when it was not too cold and talk to them, because I was interested in propagandizing them politically and also I was interested in the women. I would meet women there and be introduced to them, or I would introduce myself, as I was pretty much over my hang-up by then. So when it got cold and dark in the park they would go to the cafeteria a block away and I would go with them.

I wasn't working at the time, I was a paid revolutionist for a year but I got very little money, and I would be ashamed not to have anything on my check when I left the cafeteria and had to pass the cashier and give her my check.

So whenever I went to the cafeteria, I would order coffee or cake and pay the cashier for it, although I really couldn't afford it and could have easily lived without it. Then I said to myself, 'Shit, this is stupid! Why should I care what the cashier thinks of me?' I was working on myself to acquire a philosophy of happiness, including a philosophy of non-shame. I realized even then that shame was the essence of much human disturbance and that it was usually irrationally self-created. I figured out that I was foolishly *ashamed* not to pay the cafeteria cashier I had already got myself over my public-speaking phobia and my anxiety about approaching women, so I said, 'This is stupid! Why should I eat anything in the cafeteria and then have to pay for it when I leave? Fuck it, I don't have to! So she'll hate me!' And I convinced myself, 'If she (and my friends) hate me, let them! I never have to feel ashamed or embarrassed even if they do!'

I travelled around Manhattan at that time – I was a songwriter and was trying to sell my songs – and I often used to go to the Horn and Hardhadt cafeterias. There was a whole chain of them in New York and you went in and put nickels in the slots to get your food, so there was no cashier. I could always go the men's room or get a glass of water without reckoning with a cashier on the way out. So I always used these special cashier-free cafeterias when I wanted to go to the lavatory but didn't want to buy anything.

But I now decided I would go into every regular cafeteria I passed, and in the next couple of months I passed and deliberately entered about fifty of them. I went right in each one, took a check, went to the water fountain, got a glass of water, or went to the john, came right out, gave my check to the cashier and didn't pay anything. The cashiers looked at me and some of them said, 'You have no right to do this! You can't use our facilities without buying anything!' So I said, 'Oh, yes I can. By law, you are required to serve me, whether or not I buy anything.' You see, I had read the New York law and it clearly said that a public carrier had to take care of customers without their buying anything, unless they have a sign outside saying that there's a cover charge; and at that time only one cafeteria in the whole of New York had that kind of sign.

So I got completely over my shame by inventing and using this shame-attacking exercise. My lack of shame and embarrassment also snowballed. For after no longer feeling ashamed to confront cafeteria cashiers, I was also able to go into ordinary office buildings in New York and say to the elevator starter, 'Where's the nearest men's room in this building?' and he would say, 'Third floor' or whatever floor it was on. So I would go up to that floor, use the bathroom and come right down again. I didn't give a damn what anyone thought! Where I had previously worried about what practically everyone thought of me, I now trained myself to be quite shameless. I did a lot of other things like that – for instance, I started on self-disclosure, telling my friends about my foibles and failures and not only my successes. So I often did very specific shame-attacking exercises. Where my friends had to liquor themselves up in order to let their hair down and say and do what they really wanted to do, I rarely drank anything but soda and was much more risk-taking than they were.

W.D. So there were elements quite early in your life which we could say were the seeds of later important rational-emotive techniques?

A.E. That's right. I was going to write a book on happiness later. I wanted to educate people and show them there were rational ways of doing things, as Emerson and Bertrand Russell had said. George Santayana wrote four volumes on rationality. He was one of my favourite philosophers and he said there were rational and irrational ways of doing things – so let's do things rationally! And I figured out from reading philosophy and from monitoring my own reactions and seeing how I made myself miserable that I (and others) could be much happier if we stopped caring *too* much about what people thought of us.

W.D. Do you think there's a danger with therapists finding useful techniques in their own lives and then generalizing them to others?

A.E. Oh yes, there's a danger – I'm sure a lot of rotten therapy has been done that way. For example, therapists may find that by being angry at others and telling them off they sometimes manage to intimidate meek people and get their own way, and they feel good about that so then they teach their clients to be angry. There's a definite danger in relying too much on your own experience and feelings. But I think that because my hobby was philosophy, I was both monitoring myself *and* getting some validation through other philosophers' observations and ideas, rather than making up my useful techniques all by myself.

W.D. So you're saying that such a charge couldn't be laid at your door?

A.E. I doubt it. I suppose to some degree it could be, because for example I'm irreligious myself and live quite happily without any gods, saints or transcendental figures. So I think that it's better for people to have no goddamn mysticism or religion, and you could say that's a prejudice. But I think many of my ideas have been endorsed by philosophers who wrote books on happiness, practicality and rationality. Starting with several ancient Asian thinkers, and continuing with Epicurus, Epictetus, Marcus Aurelius, Spinoza, Kant, Bentham and other later philosophers, the philosophy of human happiness has a long history. I read all these thinkers, thought over what they wrote, and often said to myself,

'Well, that sounds good. I'll try that!' So I kept experimenting with various ideas in my own day-to-day life, and built a personal philosophy, from age 19 onward, of stubbornly refusing to make myself miserable.

W.D. Just listening to you, it sounds as if you still have a high degree of enthusiasm for the field of psychotherapy. Is that true?

A.E. Oh yes, I still have a high degree of enthusiasm. I believe that most people have an innate ability to change, to stop making themselves miserable, and that they can be helped through sensible and scientific therapy to enhance that ability, and then proceed to be quite, though not perfectly, happy.

W.D. Now you've been in the field of psychotherapy for over forty-five years, practising and refining RET, seeing large numbers clients, writing and giving workshops – there's been a fair amount of repetition in all this, hasn't there? How on earth do you maintain your high level of enthusiasm?

A.E. Because I dislike inefficiency and I like problem-solving. My father and brother were champion chess players and as a child I quite good at chess, too. I was also excellent at bridge and other card games. But I thought that all these games, including chess, had a limited number of permutations and combinations that you could learn and remember, and that was it. Even when you are good at these games, you are still limited, whereas trying to help people be less miserable and happier is still problem-solving but is much less limited. I started by trying to solve my own problems and then I went on to other people's. Naturally I don't always succeed, but I'm sure that my enthusiasm and my belief that my clients can make themselves considerably less disturbed and enjoy themselves more helps me establish rapport with them and encourages them to work to change themselves.

W.D. One of the questions that crops up among therapists is how to avoid professional burn-out. How do you manage that?

A.E. I avoid it in several ways. One is that the energy I use is not exactly physical energy. If I had to stand up all day and talk to people, I would be a basket case. My body is OK, but it's rather thin and frail, so I hardly spend a lot of time running around the block. If I had to travel from place to place each day doing therapy, I would be in trouble. But I can sit – or practically lie – in my comfortable lounge chair, usually with my eyes closed (because my eyes easily get tired), and I can listen very actively and talk a lot during my eighty or more individual therapy sessions each week.

So I don't find my usual fourteen-hour work-day very tiring. I start at nine in the morning and finish at eleven in the evening – but I often find that I feel fresher during my last two than during my first two hours of therapy. My five group sessions each week are more strenuous, but I find them even more interesting than my individual sessions and therefore not too tiring.

My all-day workshops, which go from about 9.00 a.m. to 4.30 p.m., do get a little tiring towards the end. But I only do them about once a week, usually out of town so I can easily manage that.

When I am at the Institute in New York, I usually work from 9.00 a.m. to 11.00 p.m., mostly with individual clients but when I finish, I am often very wide awake and full of energy, more so than Janet, my partner, who works a few less hours than I do and who is younger than I. But I rest in my comfortable lounge chair most of the day, feel nice and comfortable, and am mainly thinking and problem-solving. I don't find – when you're not anxious about it – that that requires a lot of energy. You see, if I were anxious like many therapists are – they see five or six clients a day and they tell me how tired they get – I'd probably be quite burned out! They worry too much about how well they are doing and therefore take their cases *too* seriously. I have a great advantage over many therapists in that if I fail to help some clients, I'm never going to depress or kill myself. So I lose a client! So I don't get some to change! So they keep coming back and back and I still don't help them! Well, I still don't get discouraged. I may say to myself, 'Oh shit, I don't think I'm ever going to get anywhere with this person.' But I only make myself feel sorry and disappointed and not anxious or depressed.

W.D. In other words, you don't make yourself disturbed about it. But also you've written elsewhere about your inherited tendency to be active and not to become tired.

A.E. My mother and father were both very active, my mother till the age of 93, and my father till he died at 80. So they weren't passive, inert people. I have the high energy level of both my parents, as long as I don't do too much physical exercise. I'm diabetic and I have rotten feet now, though in the old days I walked a lot and did very well with that kind of exercise. But these days, I find it too tiring. So I exercise relatively little.

However, I get bored shitless being passive! I often say that I was raised every summer on the beaches of Wildwood, New Jersey, for eight years and one year in Atlantic City, but I detest beaches, they're too goddam hot. You just lie there and who needs it? If I want to read, I'm certainly not going to read on a beach! Also, being in the country doesn't thrill me, even sight-seeing doesn't thrill me. None of those things do, they're too passive. I can and do enjoy plays and movies, but not quite as much as I enjoy being creatively active, and that includes my writing. I always intended to be a writer, since the age of 13 and I like writing a lot more than reading or seeing a play.

W.D. Finally, if you had the opportunity to do it all over again, are there a couple of things you would change about your career as a therapist, writer and educator?

A.E. Well, there are things I might do to gain status. For example, I almost became a psychiatrist, because I was going to Teachers College, Columbia, and I decided I would go to medical school and become a psychiatrist. I had it all plotted and schemed because I didn't have the money for medical school – in those days you had to put up something like 10,000 dollars. I had worked to pay my own way through graduate school, as we didn't have any funds and my family didn't help me. So I decided that first of all I would go and take a few courses in chemistry. I only had a Bachelors of Business Administration qualification and had to take some science courses because otherwise they wouldn't let me in medical school.

I planned to get my PhD from Columbia and then tell their school of medicine that I wanted to take a couple of courses in medicine to help me as a psychologist. They would probably have let me take them as long as I already had a PhD. Then I planned to show my professors how good I was and would somehow wangle my way into becoming one of the few people who ever got through Columbia College of Physicians and Surgeons on a part-time basis. I had it all plotted and schemed to follow that unique plan – then I went to NYU and took a course in chemistry and it was really childish. I was good at math, but I had to memorize many chemical formulae and tables. The way they organized the lab work was that they wouldn't let you do it by yourself, you had to have a lab partner who was more of a hindrance than a help; and I found most of the course boring.

At the same time, I was doing research on hermaphrodites for my first published article. So I had the choice between continuing with the chemistry course or continuing the article on hermaphrodites and really doing a good job on it. So I said to myself, 'The hell with it! It's too much of a bore going through all this pre-medical work. I think I can become well enough known as a psychologist without needing to become a psychiatrist.' The problem was that in those days, psychiatrists had all the prestige and psychologists were second-rate citizens.

W.D. But presumably, looking back, a rational Albert Ellis would say, 'Well, that was LFT – low frustration tolerance – and perhaps if I had put up with the short-term hassle for the long-term gain, then that may have been the better choice?'

A.E. Yes, and also I gambled. Because I didn't *know* I would become well known as a psychologist, I just assumed that I probably would because I had energy and was going to write many articles. And, in fact, I became well known before I became a rational therapist, because I wrote a famous paper as part of my PhD thesis on personality tests – paper and pencil tests. I ripped up most of the popular tests of the day – especially the Bernreuter Test – and quickly became very well known in the field of psychology. I thus first became an authority on personality tests rather than on the fields I was really interested in – psychotherapy and sex. So giving up my plan to sneak into medical school was a gamble, and if I had to do it over, especially today when biology has become more and more important in psychotherapy, I might become a psychiatrist rather than a psychologist and still go on to found RET and do the other things that I have done.

W.D. Can I just pick up one or two things you mentioned there? It seems from what you were saying that to become well known was quite important to you.

A.E. Yes, because don't forget that this was 1946 and I was already doing some private sex therapy and was writing on sex, so one of the reasons I wanted the prestige was not just because I wanted to become famous for its own sake, but because it would have given me the authority to be able to promulgate some of my liberal sex views.

W.D. So rather than wanting to become well known for ego reasons, you thought it would be a good instrumental way of spreading your ideas?

A.E. Yes and, especially if I had been a psychiatrist, I would have got away more easily with my liberal sex views than if I were just a psychologist.

W.D. So that's one thing you would have perhaps done differently. Is there anything else?

A.E. Well, if I had the whole thing to do over, once I had formulated

RET I might well go for more of an academic career. Because the great advantage of academia is that you have many eager students available to you; and if you are a good professor, especially a top professor with prestige, you can have a large number of students who flock to you to get their degrees. Then you can teach them RET and do considerable psychotherapy research with them. So if I had it to do over again, I might well pick academia for that reason, even though being an academic is often a royal pain in the ass. However, considering my liberal sex views, I (like Bertrand Russell) would have had trouble getting academic tenure. Thus, when I tried to get a job as an assistant professor after I resigned as Chief Psychologist of the State of New Jersey at the beginning of 1952, I discovered that doing so was very difficult. Because of my sex book, *The Folklore of Sex*, I was too liberal for most university psychology departments, including Columbia University and City College of New York, of both of which I was already a distinguished graduate. With my writings and my professional and public lectures on sex, I had already created a bad reputation for academia by my sexual writings, even though I had an outstanding reputation for writings and talks on personality tests.

W.D. But did you subsequently receive any offers of academic positions?

A.E. Yes, I have had several academic positions as adjuncts. For a while, before they became poorer, I was an adjunct professor at Rutgers University and at USIU in San Diego, and I am still an adjunct professor at Kansas State College in Pittsburg and at the University of Puerto Rico. So I get these adjunct positions, but they are unlike a regular professorial position, because you don't teach regular classes, you just teach workshops.

W.D. So again, the main reason for wanting to go into academia is that it would have given you a better platform for the promulgation of your ideas?

A.E. That's right. If I were to do things over again, I might, with hindsight, have emphasized RET and not my sexual views, because in the old days the universities wouldn't accept me on their staff because of my sex attitudes. My own university, Teachers College, Columbia, was horrified because of my notoriety in this area, so even when I asked to be an instructor there, while I was building up my psychotherapy practice, they flatly – and prudishly – turned me down.

W.D. But it seems to me, in conclusion, that even though you didn't become a psychiatrist or an academic, the one thing you certainly succeeded in doing is getting your views across!

A.E. Yes, but that's largely because I'm still a propagandist – not just a therapist with original views. There have probably been many therapists with distinct views whom we have never heard of because they didn't write much and they didn't try to get their views across. I write and I speak a great deal, and because of my speaking, my workshops and my writings, I get my views over. Now we could say, although we'll never know for sure, that if I had been primarily an academician I might never have even started RET, because I originated it as a result of clinical work and developed it almost entirely through clinical practice. Later, there was favourable outcome research on RET and CBT, these two sister therapies. So I might never have got around to the theory and practice of RET if I had been less of a clinician. Similarly with Freud. He always tried to get academic positions and never really succeeded. Now suppose he had been a top professor – he might never have started psychoanalysis! So it may all have worked out for the best. Most of the originators of popular psychotherapies – including Freud, Adler, Jung, Horney, Berne, Perls, Klein and myself – have primarily been clinicians, not academics.

If I had originated RET today, I might well, in order to promulgate it and research it, have tried to be a top professor of psychiatry or of psychology. But I thoroughly enjoy being mainly a practising clinician – so I might well choose to be that all over again!

W.D. Well, I think that's a good place to end. Thank you, Albert Ellis.

FURTHER READING

For those who wish to read further about the work of Albert Ellis, the following books are suggested.

Books by Albert Ellis

Ellis, A. (1962) *Reason and Emotion in Psychotherapy*, Secaucus, NJ: Citadel. This was Ellis's first major work on RET and continues to be his most-cited book. Some chapters are still relevant today, but the book is mainly of historical value.

Ellis, A. (1985) *Overcoming Resistance: Rational-Emotive Therapy with Difficult Clients*, New York: Springer. This book represents a complete statement of Ellis's views on understanding resistance in psychotherapy and what can be done to overcome it.

Ellis, A. and Abrahms, E. (1978) *Brief Psychotherapy in Medical and Health Practice*, New York: Springer. This book represents Ellis's major statement on brief therapy. Although written for medical and health practitioners, its application is much broader.

Ellis, A. and Dryden, W. (1987) *The Practice of Rational-Emotive Therapy*, New York: Springer. This book considers the practice of RET in the major therapeutic modalities (e.g. individual therapy, couple therapy, family therapy, group therapy and sex therapy).

Ellis, A. and Yeager, R. J. (1989) *Why Some Therapies don't Work: The Dangers of Transpersonal Psychology*, Buffalo, NY: Prometheus. This is a stinging and controversial critique of approaches to psychotherapy associated with the fourth force of psychology, transpersonal psychology.

Ellis, A., McInerney, J. F., DiGiuseppe, R. and Yeager, R. J. (1988) *Rational-Emotive Therapy with Alcoholics and Substance Abusers*, New York: Pergamon. This book is a clear, concise treatment guide to helping clients with problems of addictions.

Ellis, A., Sichel, J. L., Yeager, R. J., DiMattia, D. J. and DiGiuseppe, R. (1989) *Rational-Emotive Couples Therapy*, New York: Pergamon. This book gives a clear account of how to use RET to help couples in trouble.

Books on Albert Ellis

Bernard, M. E. and DiGiuseppe, R. (eds) (1989) *Inside Rational-Emotive Therapy: A Critical Appraisal of the Theory and Therapy of Albert Ellis*, San Diego, Calif.: Academic Press. This book contains critical appraisals of the theory and therapy of Albert Ellis written by leading authorities on psychotherapy who are *not* exponents of RET. In the final chapter Ellis responds to his critics.

Dryden, W. (ed.) (1990) *The Essential Albert Ellis: Seminal Writings in Psychotherapy*, New York: Springer. This book contains fourteen seminal writings by Ellis on the theory and practice of RET.

Wiener, D. N. (1988) *Albert Ellis: Passionate Skeptic*, New York: Praeger. The first biography on Albert Ellis to be published. The book contains much interesting material not previously available in published form. However, it has not met with unreserved approval from Albert Ellis and other RET therapists.

Yankura, J. and Dryden, W. (1990) *Doing RET: Albert Ellis in Action*, New York: Springer. This book is the first to present a critique of Albert Ellis's way of conducting psychotherapy based on tapes of his actual work with clients.

REFERENCES

Bandler, R. and Grinder, J. (1975) *The Structure of Magic* (2 vols), Palo Alto, Calif: Science and Behavior Books.

Bandura, A. (1969) *Principles of Behavior Modification*, New York: Holt, Rinehart & Winston.

Beck, A. T. (1967) *Depression: Clinical, Experimental and Theoretical Aspects*, New York: Hoeber.

Bernard, M. E. and DiGiuseppe, R. (eds) (1989) *Inside Rational-Emotive Therapy*, San Diego, Calif: Academic Press.

DiMattia, D. J. and Lega, L. (eds) (1990) *Will the Real Albert Ellis Please Stand Up?*, New York: Institute for Rational-Emotive Therapy.

Dryden, W. (1989) Albert Ellis: an efficient and passionate life, *Journal of Counseling and Development* 67: 539–46.

Dryden, W. (ed.) (1990) *The Essential Albert Ellis*, New York: Springer.

Ellis, A. (1945) The sexual psychology of human hermaphrodites, *Psychosomatic Medicine* 7: 108–25.

Ellis, A. (1946) The validity of personality questionnaires, *Psychological Bulletin* 43: 385–440.

Ellis, A (1950) An introduction to the principles of scientific psychoanalysis, *Genetic Psychology Monographs* 41: 147–212.

Ellis, A. (1951) *The Folklore of Sex*, New York: Boni/Doubleday.

Ellis, A. (1952) What is normal sex behavior? *Complex* 8: 41–51 (revised in A. Ellis and R. Brancale (eds) *The Psychology of Sex Offenders*, Springfield, Ill: Charles C. Thomas, 1956).

Ellis, A. (1953) Is the vaginal orgasm a myth?, in A. P. Pillay and A. Ellis (eds) *Sex, Sociology and the Individual*, Bombay: International Journal of Sexology.

Ellis, A. (1954) *The American Sexual Tragedy*, New York: Twayne.

Ellis, A. (1955) New approaches to psychotherapy techniques, *Journal of Clinical Psychology Monograph Supplement* 11: 1–53.

Ellis, A. (1957) *How to Live with a Neurotic*, New York: Crown.

Ellis, A. (1958) *Sex without Guilt*, Secaucus, NJ: Lyle Stuart.

Ellis, A. (1960) *The Art and Science of Love*, Secaucus, NJ: Lyle Stuart.

Ellis, A. (1962) *Reason and Emotion in Psychotherapy*, Secaucus, NJ: Citadel.

Ellis, A. (1963a) *Sex and the Single Man*, Secaucus, NJ: Lyle Stuart.
Ellis, A. (1963b) *The Intelligent Woman's Guide to Manhunting*, Secaucus, NJ: Lyle Stuart.
Ellis, A. (1965) *The Case for Sexual Liberty*, Tucson, AZ: Seymour Press.
Ellis, A. (1968) *Is Objectivism a Religion?*, Secaucus, NJ: Lyle Stuart.
Ellis, A. (speaker) (1972a) *Conquering Low Frustration Tolerance* (cassette recording), New York: Institute for Rational-Emotive Therapy.
Ellis, A. (1972b) Helping people get better rather than merely feel better, *Rational Living* 7, 2: 2–9.
Ellis, A. (1972c) *Executive Leadership: A Rational Approach*, New York: Citadel.
Ellis, A. (1973a) *Humanistic Psychotherapy: The Rational-Emotive Approach*, New York: McGraw-Hill.
Ellis, A. (speaker) (1973b) *How to Stubbornly Refuse to be Ashamed of Anything* (cassette recording), New York: Institute for Rational-Emotive Therapy.
Ellis, A. (speaker) (1973c) *Twenty-One Ways to Stop Worrying* (cassette recording), New York: Institute for Rational-Emotive Therapy.
Ellis, A. (1975) *How to Live with a Neurotic*, rev. edn, North Hollywood, Calif: Wilshire Books.
Ellis, A. (1976) The biological basis of human irrationality, *Journal of Individual Psychology* 32: 145–68.
Ellis, A. (1977a) *Anger–How to Live With and Without it*, Secaucus, NJ: Citadel.
Ellis, A. (speaker) (1977b) *Conquering the Dire Need for Love* (cassette recording), New York: Institute for Rational-Emotive Therapy.
Ellis, A. (singer) (1977c) *A Garland of Rational Songs* (cassette recording), New York: Institute for Rational-Emotive Therapy.
Ellis, A. (1983) The philosophic implications and dangers of some popular behavior therapy techniques, in M. Rosenbaum, C. M. Franks and Y. Jaffe (eds) *Perspectives on Behavior Therapy in the Eighties*, New York: Springer.
Ellis, A. (1985) *Overcoming Resistance: Rational-Emotive Therapy with Difficult Clients*, New York: Springer.
Ellis, A. (speaker) (1986) *Effective Self-Assertion* (cassette recording no. 20307), Washington, DC: Psychology Today Tapes.
Ellis, A. (1988) *How to Stubbornly Refuse to Make Yourself Miserable about Anything – Yes, Anything!*, Secaucus, NJ: Lyle Stuart.
Ellis, A. and Becker, I. (1982) *A Guide to Personal Happiness*, North Hollywood, Calif: Wilshire Books.
Ellis, A. and Brancale, R. (eds) (1956) *The Psychology of Sex Offenders*, Springfield, Ill: Charles C. Thomas.
Ellis, A. and Cory, D. W. (1952) In defense of current sex studies, *Nation* 174: 250–2.
Ellis, A. and Dryden, W. (1987) *The Practice of Rational-Emotive Therapy*, New York: Springer.

Ellis, A. and Gullo, J. (1971) *Murder and Assassination*, Secaucus, NJ: Lyle Stuart.

Ellis, A. and Harper, R. A. (1975) *A New Guide to Rational Living*, North Hollywood, Calif: Wilshire Books.

Ellis, A. and Sagarin, E. (1967) *Nymphomania: A Study of the Oversexed Woman*, New York: Gilbert Press.

Ellis, A. and Yeager, R. J. (1989) *Why Some Therapies don't Work: The Dangers of Transpersonal Psychology*, Buffalo, NY: Prometheus.

Ellis, A., McInerney, J. F., DiGiuseppe, R. and Yeager, R. J. (1988) *Rational-Emotive Therapy with Alcoholics and Substance Abusers*, New York: Pergamon.

Ellis, A., Sichel, J. Yeager, R. J., DiMattia, D. J. and DiGiuseppe, R. (1989) *Rational-Emotive Couples Therapy*, New York: Pergamon.

Glasser, W. (1965) *Reality Therapy*, New York: Harper.

Goldfried, M. R. (1980) Toward the delineation of therapeutic change principles, *American Psychologist* 35: 991–99.

Goldfried, M. R. and Davison, G. (1976) *Clinical Behavior Therapy*, New York: Holt, Rinehart & Winston.

Haley, J. (1973) *Uncommon Therapy: The Psychiatric Techniques of Milton H. Erickson, M. D.*, New York: Norton.

Kelly, G. A. (1955) *The Psychology of Personal Constructs* (2 vols) New York: Norton.

Korzybski, A. (1933) *Science and Sanity*, Lancaster Pa: Lancaster Press.

Lazarus, A. A. (1971) *Behavior Therapy and Beyond*, New York: McGraw-Hill.

Lazarus, A. A. (1989) The practice of rational-emotive therapy, in M. E. Bernard and R. DiGiuseppe (eds) *Inside Rational-Emotive Therapy*, San Diego, Calif: Academic Press.

Mahoney, M. J. (1974) *Cognition and Behavior Modification*, Cambridge, Mass: Ballinger.

Maultsby, M. C. Jr (1971) *Handbook of Rational Self-Counseling*, Lexington, Ky: Rational Self Help Books.

Meichenbaum, D. (1971) *Cognitive Factors in Behavior Modification: Modifying what Clients Say to Themselves*, Research Report no. 25, Waterloo: University of Waterloo.

Raimy, V (1975) *Misunderstandings of the Self: Cognitive Psychotherapy and the Misconception Hypothesis*, San Francisco, Calif: Jossey-Bass.

Warga, C. (1988) Profile of psychologist Albert Ellis, *Psychology Today* September: 18–23.

Wiener, D. (1988) *Albert Ellis: Passionate Skeptic*, New York: Praeger.

Yankura, J. and Dryden, W. (1990) *Doing RET: Albert Ellis in Action*, New York: Springer.

INDEX